Still on the Farm

Copyright 2001 by Eric Bergeson
Country Scribe Publishing
4177 Country Highway 1
Fertile, MN 56540

ISBN 0-9657578-1-1

Contents

CHAPTER ONE

RELICS

Lone Trees

The occasional huge tree which stands alone in the middle of a field makes a dramatic mark on our otherwise flat landscape. I have a soft spot for those lone trees, and for whoever it was who spared them from the bulldozer.

Often it becomes obvious as I drive by that the tree was spared simply because it straddled a property line. Neither farmer knew whose tree it was, so neither felt right tearing it down. More likely, each was hoping the other would take care of it.

Other lone trees stand right out in the middle of a field, which means somebody a while back decided he was willing to farm around the thing for the next thirty years, a decision I admire.

Once they survive the bulldozer, life isn't easy for lone trees. They are likely to be hit with farm chemicals no matter which way the wind is blowing. They are more vulnerable to summer storms and winter winds than their colleagues in the woods. Passing farm equipment tears away at their roots.

In fact, most of the local lone trees I remember from childhood have died off, one by one. The lone elm have been wiped out by disease. One of my favorite lone oaks was killed by herbicide a couple of springs ago.

A lone pine tree which my grandfather planted forty years back at the intersection of the main highway and the road to our farm was burned to a crisp by the sun in the winter of

1996. It looked stone dead. But the new buds were alive, and fresh needles emerged that June. Today it is a richer green than ever before.

The toughest lone trees seem to be the cottonwoods. My nominee for the king of all lone trees in this part of the world is a majestic cottonwood that towers over the north side of Highway 108 between Pelican Rapids and I-94. It must be nearly a century old. It is perfectly proportioned and elegantly droopy, a real mammoth.

I imagine that a debate went on in the head of those clearing the land: Should we save this beautiful tree, or should we do what makes business sense? For most, the answer to the question was obvious. Make way for progress!

But others let their sentiments rule, at least one time. Every time I pass a lone tree, I think good thoughts about the nameless landowner who left a grand tree standing for the rest of us to enjoy.

Church Basements

As the countryside loses people, the old country churches close one by one. The town churches, if they remain vital, build big additions with one thing in mind: Eliminate those pesky steps.

So, another rural institution is going by the wayside: The church basement is as doomed as those sagging old barns.

The end of church basements is probably not worth getting too upset about. Those steps make things difficult for elderly churchgoers. Hotdishes and green jello will taste just as good upstairs in the carpeted addition.

But, after attending a meeting in a church basement yesterday, I got a little nostalgic about what is going away. There is a powerful smell of coffee and mold in all of those basements which crosses denominational lines. Even county and state lines.

They never got too fancy with those basements. The floors are usually tile. The bare steel posts ring when you bump into them. The paneling is cheap stuff from the seventies. The chairs are metal and make loud noises when dragged along the floor.

The acoustics are terrible. Put twenty people down there and it sounds like a thousand. Carrying on a conversation with somebody hard of hearing is an exercise in futility. Hearing aids screech and whine, unable to sort out one voice from the rest of the cacophony.

Most church basements have an old piano with ivories missing which they use for Sunday school. It was probably last tuned during the Truman administration.

For Luther League, or a funeral, or whatever, somebody usually brings a cold tuna salad containing shoe-string potatoes and celery chunks all globbed together by a jar of mayonnaise — a dish I would never eat at home, but one which is almost a sacramental part of church basement dinners.

And then there are the hotdishes, probably also on their way out. There is a bill in the Minnesota legislature to protect hotdishes at church dinners from government interference. Once the legislature gets the notion to protect something, you know it is not long for this world.

The Ladies Aid at the church down the road from our farm used to serve hotdish suppers in the basement once a month. It was a neighborhood gathering. It didn't matter if you were from that church or not. All were welcome. Those meals were sumptuous.

But the dinners were meant to raise funds, and it turned out they were costing more to make than the ladies were getting in offerings. Some old timers didn't adjust their donations for inflation. They'd throw in a dollar for a meal that would cost $8.95 anywhere else.

So the ladies decided to stick to funerals. You can't blame them. Funerals pay. But I do regret that I don't have a chance to meet with the neighbors over hotdish in a musty church basement one Wednesday evening per month.

Junk in the Woods

When you move to town, you lose your right to store things out in the woods. In the woods is where country people put things that are too good to throw but too much of a nuisance to keep in the shop or the house.

Have you noticed that country people don't have as many rummage sales as town folk? That's because they don't need to have rummage sales. When junk builds up, they just put it out in the woods.

Don't want to part with that old milk can? Put it out in the woods. Wondering what to do with that hay rake you bought for forty bucks at the auction? Put it in the woods. What about the old cookware? Nobody wants it, but it is too good to throw. Just put it in the woods.

For the past ninety years on our home place, previous generations piled their stuff out in the woods. I've been digging around back there for fun, and I feel as if I am finding buried treasure.

First, I dragged a couple of huge steel wheels up to the yard. Dad looked at me like I was nuts. I could see the wheels triggered memories that weren't entirely pleasant.

Next, I hauled up a cultivator shovel and big saw blade. I thought they were valuable finds, but Dad just groaned and asked where I was finding all of this junk.

If you paint 'Velkommen' or some other Norwegian gibber-ish on a saw blade, it can be worth real money. But all Dad could think about was having to sharpen that blade over a hot stove in three feet of snow when he was six.

Then came some old waffle syrup cans, gas cans, sprayer tanks, cream separators, wash tubs, tractor seats, and on and on. I arranged the artifacts artistically on the cement slab.

Back in the woods for another round, I overturned a pile of copper tubing and struck gold: Utensils from my grandmother's kitchen. Cream pitchers, a china soup tureen dated 1917, pewter salt shakers, and a metal cup engraved with my grandmother's maiden name.

Deeper back was a threshing machine, the rusted body of a Model A, and the unrecognizable remains of the 1933 Plymouth that Grandma rolled in the ditch on the way to the county fair. When she rolled the car, there had been several trays of fresh raspberries in the back seat. Imagine the mess.

Now all of this rusted junk sits out on the slab. Everybody except Dad thinks its real neat. Nobody wants any of it, but they all agree that it is worth keeping somewhere.

So, I suspect the pile will sit there for a few weeks before Dad gets sick of the mess, waits until I am gone for the day, and hauls it back to the woods. After all, stuff like that is too good to throw.

Rollag's Steamers

Few annual events in this area are as much fun as the Steam Threshers Reunion in Rollag, MN. They still call the gathering a 'reunion,' even though the number of people who remember actual threshing is fast dwindling.

To those of us from the northwest corner of Minnesota, Rollag is little more than a bump on the road to the Cities. I don't know if you can even buy gas there any more.

But come Labor Day weekend, tens-of-thousands of people make a pilgrimage to the fields outside of the tiny village to watch as the mechanical dinosaurs awake from hibernation to lumber around the grounds for a few days.

When they are fired up, the old steamers seem alive. They hiss and puff, then coast along silently. I can't imagine what it was like for people at the turn of the century to see one of those monsters coming down the road for the first time.

Under the hood of a modern vehicle is an incomprehensible mess of wires and tubes. You need a degree from a tech school to begin to know what is going on.

But everything is out in the open on those old steamers. The gears, the chains, the coal, the firebox, the clickers and the clackers, the flywheels, nothing is under a hood. Even a mechanical idiot like myself can figure out what many of the parts were meant to do.

Today, famous inventors invent things the average person can't appreciate. They write new software, or develop new chemicals and drugs. Normal people use their inventions, but we'll never figure out how they function. If they work, we're happy. When they don't, we shrug and call up an expert.

But as the steamers go by at the parade in Rollag, one can not only watch the many parts at work, but you can almost see the wheels spinning in the heads of the long dead inventors as they tried to outdo each other. One tractor will feature a gadget which will be slightly improved on the next tractor, which will be even more streamlined on a steamer down the row.

Those inventors were real show-offs. I suspect they were well aware that no hood would hide their craftsmanship. They worked to build machines which not only did the job, but were beautiful to watch in operation.

The old inventors succeeded, if the crowds which flock to Rollag each Labor Day are any indication. No computer programmer will be lucky enough to have thousands of people mesmerized by his work decades after his death.

Uncle Orville's Old Baler

After the county fair leaves town, we enter into the bittersweet dog days of summer. The birds sound a bit tired, and crickets have replaced frogs as the chief noisemakers outside the window at night. In late July, the grain fields turn from green to tan almost overnight.

These late summer sounds–the crickets, the constant whir of the house fan, the drone of a Twins game on the radio–bring back powerful memories of childhood.

In late summer during childhood, PeeWee baseball was over, Bible camp was a fading memory, and the first back-to-school fliers reared their ugly heads in the mailbox. The Twins were usually 25 games out of first place by August, but I often stayed up until 1 a.m. to catch some meaningless game on the west coast. I didn't want to miss a single hit by Rod Carew.

One vital sound has disappeared from the nostalgic late summer mix: The clunkety-clunk of my uncle Orville's old baler as he baled the alfalfa on our farm. In those long summers between grades in elementary school, there was nothing I enjoyed more than to run a couple of windrows over from the baler and watch the show.

That was before round balers. Round balers make no interesting sounds and are a bore to watch. They move too fast to follow on foot. But those old clackety-clack balers with hundreds of moving parts were a symphony of bangs, clicks and thumps.

The gadgets which cut the bale, tied the twine, and kicked the bale out the back mesmerized me. I could run along side the baler for hours without getting tired. The heavy smell of fresh alfalfa intoxicated me, and I had a cud of it in my mouth at all times.

Cousin Tom drove the old tractor while Uncle Orville grabbed the fresh bales off the baler with his shiny steel bale hook. He stacked the bales on a little trailer in stooks, pyramids made up of ten bales each. When the trailer was full, he would pull a lever and the stook would slide off and be left behind.

I jogged with the baler until the sun set and Tom turned on the tractor's lights. Then I knew it was time to run home, eat some cereal, and get to bed.

While lying in bed in the cool basement, I could hear the faint thump, thump of Uncle Orville's baler as it crawled around the field. The rhythm lulled me to sleep.

When a city cousin came to the farm for a visit once, his first question was, "When are the bulldozers going to come so they can build houses here?" In his mind, all woods and fields were doomed to development.

Thank goodness, the bulldozers never came. For that reason, the Minnesota countryside was not only a great place to grow up, but still is a pretty good place to be, square bales or round.

Road Ditches

Mid-summer is when they start mowing the road ditches. I guess the idea is that you don't want all those weeds and grasses to cause the roads to drift in next winter. Mowing the ditches in summer saves on the snow plow in the winter.

Few people realize that road ditches often harbor a greater variety of plants than can be found in most gardens. Although the roadside always looks nice and neat after they mow, I sometimes wish they'd let the ditches be for as long as possible so we could enjoy the flora.

Just today, I saw a pink wild rose, a white wild rose, some yarrow, several Queen Anne's lace, and many other wild plants I can't name, all in a single ditch.

If you get real lucky, you can find a lady slipper plant in the ditch. The lady slipper is the state flower, so if you touch one, a beeper goes off in St. Paul and they send somebody out to arrest you right away.

However, the man who mows for the county is immune from prosecution, and he mows down everything—from roses to lady slippers—without fear of punishment.

During the countless thousands of hours I spent on the school bus as a child, I often looked out the window and watched the road ditches go by. I imagined that the bus had a sickle mower attached to it, and that the grass fell nicely to the ground as the bus passed.

They don't use sickle mowers anymore. They have those

grinders which do a better job, but which aren't nearly as mesmerizing to watch. There's nothing like an old sickle mower slicing through the grass and laying it neatly down.

Not every part of the country has road ditches. In Arizona, they just pave the desert without building up the road. No ditches there. When it rains, the water just runs over the road.

In Georgia, some of the old roads actually have sunk below the level of the surrounding fields. The road itself is the only ditch.

Ditches aren't all good. The biggest fear I had when I was learning to drive was that I would go in the ditch. The ultimate driving failure was ending up in the ditch.

When I got home way too late in high school, Dad would be waiting up. His main worry? That I was upside down in the ditch. As long as I wasn't in the ditch, all was okay.

But ditches were a blast as a child. The ditch banks made for great climbing on my little motorcycle. Popping out of the ditch onto the highway with the Honda 50 was as thrilling as it was stupid.

In sixth grade, I found a full beer can in the ditch. What a thrill! I didn't dare drink it, but I did pour it out and drink in the smell, which reminded me of a Twins game at old Metropolitan Stadium.

I must be getting old. I drive too slowly to worry about going in the ditch. My motorcycle days are over. The enjoyment I get out of ditches nowadays comes when I find a wild rose growing there.

Good Bread

One of life's great mysteries: Why do we put up with such terrible bread in this country? Bread is the basic food of life, yet the average loaf of white bread you get at grocery stores is a tasteless, textureless travesty.

It nauseates me to think of the quality of the bread we were served at the school cafeteria as children. Gummy white goo covered with cold globs of butter. If you toast the stuff and cover it in cinnamon and sugar, it becomes a little more interesting, but only a little.

We have the best cars in the world, the most television channels, the best baseball teams. As a country we overflow with riches, yet to find a decent loaf of bread you have to search high and low.

During the Cold War, our propagandists often pointed to our supermarkets as evidence of the superiority of our capitalist system. Look at the great variety of food the average person has at his disposal in this country, they said.

Yet, in most of those supermarkets there wasn't a single loaf of bread that could hold a candle to the loaves eaten by the poorest Russian workers. Nobody ever told us that.

The Russians know how to make bread. So do the Poles. I spent a spring in Poland just after the communists fell. The most pleasant surprise of my trip was the quality of Polish bread. Due to government subsidies and the crazy exchange rate, each loaf cost less than a penny.

Heavy, chewy crusts. Soft insides, sometimes fluffy, sometimes heavy. You had to work to chew the stuff, but you knew you had eaten something of substance when you were finished.

The daily bread would arrive at drab Polish grocery stores at about 5:30 am. Yes, there were bread lines, but mainly because people wanted their bread fresh and it was good enough to justify standing in line. I stood there with them.

The long-suffering peoples of Eastern Europe have put up with depravations of every sort over the centuries, but one thing they insist upon is quality bread.

When I heard two years ago that a colony of Russians had moved into northwestern Minnesota, my first thoughts were selfish: I wonder if any of them know how to make Russian bread?

Stupid question. It wasn't one day after I asked one of our new Russian neighbors about their bread that they drove up into our yard with a big round loaf for me to sample.

A couple of days back, I saw an ad for a bakery which carried 'old world' bread. What a great surprise! I made a sixty mile round trip to pick up several loaves of German rye bread and some other goodies. It was worth it.

Perhaps with the help of recent immigrants and with more of our local people traveling the world, we will eventually see the light in this country and improve the state of our bread.

When that happens, we can move on to tackle the equally pressing problem of our tepid, tasteless, watery beer.

Canning

Have we lost our heritage? August used to be the time of year when the womenfolk would can tomatoes, apple pickles, bread and butter pickles, beet pickles, ground cherries, plums and berries.

In the old days, they even canned meat. When fresh peaches and apricots were in season at the store, they bought and canned them. They made gooseberry pie. Green tomato relish. Even watermelon pickles. After deep freezers came in, they froze corn, peas and beans.

Times have changed. So far this year, I have heard of one homemaker who is putting up anything. She's making salsa. My grandmother would never have approved of such a thing, I'll guarantee you that.

Canning used to be economically necessary. Now it's not. Food is cheap. Fresh fruit and veggies are available at the store all year around. Plus, who has time to raise a garden and can?

The traditional country arrangement where the man worked in the barn while the woman slaved away in the kitchen has disappeared. Now the husband works at the Gizmo factory and the woman works nights at the nursing home.

My grandmother always canned. And canned. And canned. Her six children grew up and left home, but her canning habits remained constant. When we visited, there would be plenty of sauces, relishes and pickles. More than we could eat.

Grandma labeled each jar with first-aid tape. On the tape

was written the year the item was canned. The date was important, since Grandma insisted that we use the canned goods in chronological order.

That meant that if there was a jar of pretty, red, fresh strawberry sauce from 1983 on the shelf, it couldn't be opened until we had eaten the strawberry sauce labeled 1974, which had a sort of gray cast to it.

Unlike wine, canned goods do not improve with age. As a child I remember adding more and more cream until I could barely taste the old sauce. Later on, I learned to sneak out the door and dump the sauce in the hedge.

The backlog of canned goods just got worse as the years went on. By the time Grandma went to the nursing home, there were hundreds of jars on her shelves, some more than fifteen years old.

For the first six months that Grandma was in the home, she asked us about the canned goods every day. You are using them, aren't you? Don't let them go to waste!

Our answers weren't even remotely truthful. We felt like horrible people, but we weren't about to open up those jars of gray strawberries. And Grandma would never know.

The awful truth is, I had a hard time eating canned sauce anyway, especially groundcherry sauce. Fresh strawberry sauce was okay, but plum sauce made me choke. And I can take or leave pickles.

So, perhaps the switch to salsa isn't such a tragedy. Times change, and we change with them.

Penmanship

School children now learn keyboarding as early as elementary school. Keyboarding is a term for what they used to call typing.

In today's computer dominated world, it is only right that children become acquainted with a keyboard. Typing is a basic skill. However, one hopes that the emphasis on computers doesn't cause handwriting to be neglected.

It seems that penmanship has joined Latin on the educational dust heap. What do we write out by hand any more? Grocery lists. Little notes at the bottom of greeting cards. Checks. No reason to develop an elaborate cursive style for such simple tasks.

Penmanship has been going downhill for years, probably because it is used less often with every passing generation. The telegraph and telephone dealt the first blows to the importance of handwriting, and the typewriter didn't help either.

My grandmother, a teacher in the old one room schools, wrote beautifully. Her handwriting was an expression of her personality: Careful, dignified, deliberate, without frills.

During Grandma's generation, handwriting was still vital to everything from business to courtship. One's handwriting needed to legible, of course, but more than that, people hoped to present themselves well by making their handwriting handsome, even artistic.

By the time I went through school, handwriting had lost

much of its importance. The styles of handwriting no longer looked so dignified. Bubbly, round, cutesy handwriting became trendy, particularly amongst females. Most males were content to scratch the page like chickens might scratch the dirt.

With e-mail and computers, handwriting has become almost unnecessary. One can know a person for several months, even years, without catching a glimpse of their handwriting. Sometimes it is a shock to see the sloppy scratching of a person who seemed so conscientious.

Is handwriting a window to the soul? My grandfather thought so. During the long winter evenings, he read up on graphology, the art of handwriting analysis. Graphology may be on the order of fortune telling and horoscopes, but some of it made sense.

For example, Grandpa said that people who write very small are meticulous in all things. People whose signature features unusually large capital letters are vain. People who write way above the line are off in dreamland. People who use a circle to dot their i's—well, that was such a bad sign that Grandpa wouldn't tell me what it meant.

Whether or not it is possible to use handwriting to decipher the personality of another, we miss out on something when we communicate with computerized beeps and blips.

I received a letter from my great aunt Olive the other day. It was handwritten, of course. Sending it cost 33 cents, and required a trip to the mailbox. Unlike any e-mail, it was a keepsake as soon as it arrived.

Bald Eagle

Bald eagles were once nearly extinct. Now they are back in healthy numbers. Even though they are more common today, the sighting of one is still a special event.

Driving on a lonely country highway one recent morning, I noticed an odd-shaped glob atop a lone cottonwood at the side of the road. As I approached, I realized the glob was a bird. It appeared misshapen at first because its white head feathers were invisible against the foggy background.

I had never before seen a bald eagle up close in the wild, so I pulled my pickup onto the shoulder and stepped out. It was perfectly still. The fog was thick. And a bald eagle it was.

Sometimes I have been disappointed when seeing an animal up close which before I had only seen in pictures. The first zebra I saw in a zoo was smaller than I had imagined, and its white stripes were more a dirty yellow. Most buffalo I have seen in the wild have been mangy and ugly, far from grand, nothing like that healthy big cement buffalo near Jamestown, ND.

I remember distinctly the first moose I saw up close. It wandered into the yard. I chased it into the field with the pickup until I got stuck in the mud, at which time the moose circled the pickup as if to gloat.

That moose was sickly. Turns out, it was friendly only because it had a disease in the brain that moose get from ticks. If it had been healthy, I might never have seen it up close.

But the bald eagle perched in the mist atop that cottonwood was as grand as any animal I have ever seen, and as perfect as any bald eagle I have seen in a patriotic picture. I stood under the tree and watched as it flexed its wings, glared over the fields with its intimidating stare, and adjusted its talons on the branch. This bird truly ruled its roost.

The eagle's white head feathers were pure porcelain white, not yellowed, not mangy, but fluffy and healthy. The bird was far larger than I had imagined. Instead of being disappointed, I was awed.

After what must have only been a few seconds, but which seemed like minutes, the eagle took flight. I could hear the rustle of its wing feathers against the moist air.

I jumped in my pickup and took off. The eagle circled and flew alongside me as I sped up to fifty-five. I don't know how fast those things are supposed to fly, but the bird didn't lose ground even as I approached the speed limit.

Finally, as if he had finished his job of getting me up to speed and on my way, the eagle veered off across the wide open Red River Valley field and disappeared into the fog.

People make a lot of fun of those who fight to save this or that endangered species. But my visit with the bald eagle made me glad somebody, somewhere, sometime, stuck up for the grand birds when they were down and out.

Windstorms and Barns

When it gets hot up here, its just a roll of the dice which farms and towns will get pummeled by storms after nightfall. As the clouds billow up during the evenings of those humid days, you know the night is gonna shake, rattle and roll.

Forget tornadoes. Straight winds do one hundred times more damage to our area than twisters. Up and down the entire region, trees lean to the east as the result of this or that big wind storm. There have been too many bad storms to count over the past twenty years.

The morning after a storm, rumors spread in the jam-packed cafes of flipped boxcars, twisted grain bins, wrecked pontoons, roofless pole barns, and of the poor trucker from Mississippi whose rig blew over on highway 200.

Windstorms leave deep scars on the landscape, and perhaps even deeper scars on people. When a windstorm knocked over the twenty cottonwoods which surrounded my grandparents' house in 1987, Grandpa said, "this isn't home anymore," and joined Grandma in the nursing home that very week.

"We had that windstorm, you know," people say, without saying which one, or when it was. Doesn't matter, you know what they mean.

Storms destruct the familiar. There are few things people value more than secure and familiar surroundings. Storms rip up our little worlds, and such violence goes hard on people's sense of well-being.

A cheerful heroism often follows a storm. Neighbors help neighbors, chainsaws buzz, pay loaders roar. All of the activity can perk people up for a time. But once the bustle dies down, there is little left but a sad sense that things will never be the same.

A windstorm means that where there once was deep shade, there is now bare ground. Where there once was an old barn, there is now a pile of debris. Where there once was a dignified grove of trees, there is now a tangled mess.

Barns are the saddest casualties of storms, it seems to me. Houses, pole sheds and garages will be rebuilt, and if they aren't it is usually no loss to society at large. Trees take time, but they can and will come back.

But when an old barn is blown over, it is lost for good, not just to the owners, but to the rest of us who have had the pleasure of driving past the charming relic for the past decades.

In Europe, they would rebuild the downed barns for historic purposes, or just because they looked nice. We don't do that here, at least yet.

In fact, after Hitler ordered the complete destruction of every historic building in Warsaw in 1944, the Poles spent the next thirty years rebuilding the city exactly as it had been before the war. Using old paintings and photographs, they reconstructed castles, palaces and churches by the dozen down to the finest detail. Take that, Adolf.

Perhaps someday some enlightened soul around here will put up a grand dairy barn, not for cows or horses, but just for old time's sake. We can't always let the wind win.

CHAPTER TWO

OBSERVANCES

Golden Anniversary

My friends Herman and Hilda Larson celebrated their fiftieth wedding anniversary at Skaldebakken Lutheran Church last Sunday.

I deliberately showed up an hour after the program was scheduled to start, hoping to miss the mushy stuff. No such luck. There was still an hour left of poems, tributes and testimonials. The skit about their courtship was probably too accurate for Herman and Hilda's liking, although the rest of the crowd roared.

Hilda was enjoying herself, but Herman looked as if he was in pain. He was recently diagnosed with VDD (Voluntary Deafness Disorder), and the symptoms on this Sunday were particularly severe.

Herman sat with a little forced grin on his face, not reacting at all to the circus arranged by their daughter Nancy, who swooped in from Anoka Friday afternoon with the force of a March blizzard.

The program was almost bearable until the new minister got up and asked for the audience to share reminiscences and remembrances of Herman and Hilda. Dead silence. Everybody was thinking ahead to the food. And what stories were there, anyway?

I wanted to tell about the only time I heard Hilda say anything nice about Herman, the time he had his heart attack and just about died, when she admitted that she would miss him because "He's not a bad guy."

But I kept my mouth shut. As did everybody else, except for the minister who finally broke the silence by offering a long tribute to Herman and Hilda's "enduring faith," something which was news to most people in the audience.

"They sure make a fuss," Herman said to me afterwards in the basement. It looked like his suit itched terribly. The collar on his shirt was two sizes too large. He clearly couldn't wait for Monday morning when he could put on his overalls and go putter around the shop.

It wasn't so bad for Hilda. She reveled in the compliments on her hair and her corsage. For once, she didn't have to work in the kitchen. "I better enjoy being lazy this time," she said with a laugh. "Next time, it will be my funeral!"

Once everyone finished eating, things got a bit more relaxed. Herman ambled over to a dark corner full of men. His hearing disorder improved. They discussed crops, even though none of them still farm.

Nancy cooled her jets and joined a gabfest back in the kitchen. The grandkids strapped their offspring into car seats and headed back to the suburbs. The minister issued some final unctions and ascended to his reserved parking spot. The crowd dwindled down to old neighbors.

Once again, Herman and Hilda had endured.

Thanksgiving

Thanksgiving means turkey and dressing to many people. For me, however, it means struggling to get a little bit of sleep in a relative's basement somewhere in the Cities.

I don't care which relative it is, I usually end up on the hide-a-bed in the basement. That is fine, but hide-a-beds aren't meant for human use. They are meant to injure people's backs so permanently that they never come for another visit.

Before even trying to get comfortable in the hide-a-bed, I have to deal with all of the clocks. Most of my aunts collect clocks. They make sure to wind them up right before company comes.

I do what I must to sleep. I stick toothpicks in the mechanisms of wind-up clocks to silence their ticking. I have pulled out clock batteries. I have tied knots in the weights of a cuckoo clock to shut it up until morning.

Over the years I have been kept awake by clocks, by pipes squeaking, sinks dripping, mice chewing, fridges making ice, uncles snoring upstairs, and water softeners regenerating. But this Thanksgiving threw me a new curve.

Once again, I was trying to sleep in a basement somewhere in the Cities. For once, the bed wasn't so bad, and the pipes had calmed down. Once I figured out how to disconnect the rattling dehumidifier, I was ready to sleep.

But then I heard a beep. And another beep. For about an hour, I tried to get to sleep between the beeps, only to have the next beep wake me up right as I was drifting into dreamland.

I decided to attack the problem scientifically. I stood in the middle of the room facing one direction and waited for the beep. It seemed to be behind me, so I stood in the middle of that part of the room and waited for the next beep. With each beep, I got a little closer to whatever it was that was beeping.

I ended up with my nose in the laundry basket. I debated—would it be right dig through the dirty laundry of my gracious hosts?

I went ahead and dumped out the laundry. I picked off one piece of dirty laundry after another until, behold! There was a little cell phone. Who knows how the phone found its way into the laundry, but the laundry basket was "out of range," and the phone was beeping to make sure the problem didn't go unnoticed.

I shut the phone off and threw it back into the laundry basket. It was 3:30 a.m. It would only be four hours until my uncle would get up to listen to Paul Harvey at full volume.

The Meaning of Christmas

Tis the season to buy mounds of expensive junk nobody will ever use. Christmas brings out the big spender in everybody, and New Year's resolutions make the spending spree worse.

Kitchen gadgets are a big item. Most of them are worthless. What percentage of fondue pots ever get used? Most of them sit in the cupboard and collect dust. Maybe one out of 20 of those homemade noodle machines ever sees any action.

I once requested a yogurt maker for Christmas. It arrived, but I never opened the box.

The popsicle molds were a waste. The little plastic thing used to reseal open pop bottles wasn't worth the trouble.

Bread machines occasionally see some use, but ice cream makers seldom see the light of day once they get stashed under the basement stairs.

Research would likely prove that 95 percent of the food machines given as Christmas gifts are used no more than one time.

The Pentagon used to pay $700 per screwdriver, but at least they used the screwdrivers. The same can't be said for most exercise machines people buy for about the same amount of money.

"If I invest a lot of money in the machine, I will be more inclined to use it," people tell themselves. Although they seldom go for a walk outside even when the weather is beautiful, people somehow get the idea that they will spend hours on a treadmill in their basement when it is forty below.

The Christmas and New Year's holidays are times when people assess their lives. Many resolve to change for the better. But instead of changing their habits, most people buy gadgets which promise to change their lives for them.

Burn fat away without exercise! Lose weight without trying! Cook gourmet meals in five minutes! Have a flat stomach in 30 days! Grow hair on your shiny bald head! Just take this pill or buy this gadget and love and happiness will be yours.

For every deficiency people see in themselves, there is a product which promises to cure it. The human desire to accomplish great things without putting forth any effort makes these gadgets an easy sell.

Nobody seems to notice that these gadgets don't work. Exercise contraptions clog attics and storage units. Kitchen junk sells for pennies at rummage sales. Bottles of antioxidants and garlic pills stack up in the medicine drawer.

People don't learn from experience. They keep on buying. If the last gadget didn't solve their problem, they seem to think, perhaps the next one will.

Greeting Cards

Who came up with all these appreciation holidays that you have to buy cards for or else be seen as a complete jerk? According to those in the know, it is lobbyists for the greeting card industry who keep coming up with new groups of people who need appreciation.

The purpose? To sell cards to guilt-ridden people who rightly sense that they aren't always nice, and who hope to make up for their sins by scribbling their name at the bottom of a $1.95 greeting card.

Okay, Mother's Day is fine. Buying a card for Mom is a nice thing. Flowers for Mom are a good thing. Moms like appreciation, and if the state of the world is so sorry we have to set aside a day for mothers to get any credit, so be it.

But Father's Day is a bit contrived. I can't imagine a Dad sitting by the phone waiting for a call from Junior on his big day. And Grandparents Day? Secretaries Day? Administrative Assistants Day? Garbage Man Day? C'mon.

There was a time, less than one hundred years ago, when sending a greeting card with a preprinted, prefabricated sentiment was seen as lazy and rude. If you had sentiments for somebody, you wrote a letter.

But then along came the Hallmark company which realized that they could profit from the extreme difficulty people have in expressing emotion.

They started printing birthday cards. People were relieved

not to have to come up with two sentences of good wishes on their own, and the cards sold like hot cakes.

Next were Christmas cards. Much easier than writing a note! That was before those blasted copy machines made it possible for people to send out mass mailings of their holiday letter.

Then came sympathy cards. Is there any more difficult time to come up with something appropriate to say than when somebody dies? So much easier to purchase a prefabricated sentiment, scribble your name at the bottom, throw in a five dollar bill, and call it good.

Not satisfied with the billions they were making off of these understandably difficult human situations, the greeting card companies decided to create more difficult human situations.

They lobbied hard for Mother's Day, and won. More card sales. Father's Day was next.

Then things started getting ridiculous. Grandparents Day. Secretaries Day. Teachers Appreciation Day. Nobody dares say anything against these days, but the truth of the matter is that these people should be appreciated all of the time.

The notion that you can make up for a year of neglect by sending a preprinted card on a day designated by a bunch of politicians for appreciation is anything but appreciation. Appreciation purchased for $1.95 is counterfeit at best.

Prom

Tis the season for after-prom parties. With a solemn sense of purpose, volunteer committees across the area busily shake down businesses and individual citizens for donations of money and goods.

The committee uses the free televisions, microwaves, and cars to bribe the high schoolers into spending their entire prom night under the watchful gaze of parents and principal in the high school gym, instead of out at the gravel pits.

The high schoolers don't seem to mind. Its just one night, after all. The free stuff is cool. The gravel pits will still be there next weekend.

I am glad the kids can have a nice party, and I don't begrudge them the free consumer gadgets. I wouldn't sell my dignity and freedom for any less.

But what messages do these parties send to the kids? Aren't there bigger reasons not to drink beer at the pits than the possibility of a free television or some tanning tokens?

If it were me, I would begin to wonder: Just what is it I am missing out on that justifies thousands of dollars worth of prizes to bribe me not to do it? I would get very curious.

I would gladly take the free television on prom night, but I would become more determined than ever to find out just what I was missing. Maybe even the next weekend. Or after graduation. Or on July 4th at the lake. Or at the state tournament. But I would find out.

This prom thing has gone completely nuts. People spend hundreds of dollars on tuxedos and dresses and limos for their children, whether they can afford them or not. Mothers breathlessly gossip about who is going with whom. Parents get more involved in the hoopla than the kids, it seems.

In fact, if it weren't for the parents, I think the whole prom concept would die a merciful death. Not just the after prom bash, but the whole sordid, elitist, wasteful affair. Most teenage kids have more sense than their parents. They would quickly put all of that money to better use.

However, the kids know that if they go along with this prom thing they'll pretty much have a free ride the rest of the year. They realize that the parental belief that prom is the only night of the year where their children's innocence is at risk is a delusion well worth preserving.

Meanwhile, the parents go on in their dream world. They assume their children are dying to do all of the evil things they did themselves on their prom nights, and they hypocritically try to prevent it.

More likely, the parents are trying to prevent their children from doing the wild things they wished they would have done themselves, but didn't have the guts.

Graduation Receptions

It is almost time for graduation. For the parents of graduates, that means it is time to get ready for the big reception. Time to finish all of the household projects that have been put off for the last seventeen years.

Most people go way overboard preparing for their graduation reception. One woman I know is fighting to get her cupboards reorganized in time for the big day. As if anybody will care.

Others start remodeling, reshingling, redoing the shrubs, and putting in new carpet about a week before the reception. Late night trips to Menard's, frantic calls to overworked electricians–if they're lucky, the mess will get cleaned up a few minutes before the first guest arrives.

Most graduates don't care if their house is fixed up or not. But to parents, the prospect of teachers, neighbors and community leaders marching into their living room fills them with terror.

When the big day comes, most visitors don't even notice the new carpet. They are too busy rushing from house to house stuffing themselves with cake and punch.

If parents of graduates really wanted to make an impression on their guests, they wouldn't waste one minute remodeling. Instead, they would teach their graduates how to shake hands with the guests, smile, and engage the visitors in polite conversation.

Many high school seniors seem to care more about the cash inside the cards than they do about the people who bring them. Others are more interested in the big bash at the gravel pits later that night.

I remember the most pleasant graduation reception I have ever attended. It was in a big old farmhouse. No remodeling there. In fact, it looked as if the dining room table had been cleared of newspapers just that morning. A pile of dirty laundry was visible from the landing.

But the graduate was warm and friendly, greeted all the guests, and charmed the older people. Everybody was relaxed by the informal atmosphere. A good time was had by all.

Memorial Day

Graduation and Memorial Day are back-to-back occasions, and they contrast: Graduation looks forward, Memorial Day looks back.

We are a forward-looking country with a short memory, so we prefer attending graduations to attending Memorial Day services. Celebrating the unlimited potential of fresh faced graduates takes precedence over remembering the sacrifices of the long dead.

A short national memory is not all bad. Recent wars in Eastern Europe stem in part from people trying to get revenge on each other for wrongs committed centuries ago. In the Mideast, fanatics use ancient history to justify most any kind of slaughter.

Even so, I have come to prefer Memorial Day to graduation. I think we could afford to remember the dead more than we do, and I think graduates could get by with a little less unearned adulation.

As a part of my job, I deliver planters of flowers to grave sites each Memorial Day. I have spent hours looking for particular graves, and have learned some history on the way.

For instance, there are many markers in local cemeteries for people who died in 1918. These aren't the graves of World War I veterans as one might think. The markers are for people from infancy to old age who died in the terrible flu epidemic of 1918.

How many people today even know that the epidemic happened? At least thirty million people died of the flu around the world, more than died in World War I, but no mention is made of the 1918 epidemic in high school history books.

A neighboring farm family was wiped out by that flu. Seven of the nine family members died within a month. Their farmstead still sits abandoned, the old log buildings buried under fallen trees, barely visible from the road. The family is buried in a nearby cemetery.

Why should we remember these people? Perhaps only to give us some humility. Scientists, for all of their advances, still haven't figured out the flu bug of 1918. For all we know, it could happen again.

I once took my grandfather out of the nursing home for a drive. We stopped at the cemetery in Twin Valley, his old stomping ground. Grandpa jumped out of the car and virtually ran from stone to stone.

"This is like old home week!" he said, plainly delighted to be amongst the memories of many old friends. He knew most of the people buried there.

To young graduates who are convinced of their immortality and importance, visiting a cemetery might seem like a morbid waste of time.

But I think the young could benefit from taking a trip with their grandparents through a cemetery. By seeing the graves and hearing about those buried in them, they might begin to learn the humbling but liberating lesson that life is short and that the mark we leave on this earth is small.

Meal Time

On the farm, we adhered faithfully to the following meal schedule, which I am sure is decreed somewhere in Leviticus:

Breakfast was at sunrise and was filled with greasy meats, pancakes, maybe some oatmeal.

Morning coffee was at nine-thirty and consisted of leftover pancakes rolled up with butter and sugar, or, if the pancakes were all gone, maybe a cheese sandwich.

Noon meal was called dinner and was a full meat and potatoes affair, finished off with pudding topped by whatever fresh fruit was in season. The drink, for the children at least, was nectar.

Afternoon coffee, sometimes called lunch, was at three o'clock sharp and featured fresh cookies, maybe even fresh bread.

The six o'clock meal was called supper. Supper meant a tater-tot hotdish, stroganoff, liver and onions, or something else filling and hearty. Sometimes we just ate the leftovers from dinner. They tasted even better the second time around.

Then I went to college in the suburbs. What a shock! I found that dinner had been moved to six o'clock. Noon meal consisted of croissants and salad. It was called "lunch."

Nobody had morning or afternoon coffee as an organized event, and supper was eliminated completely. When I once referred to the noon meal as dinner, the suburbanites mocked me as a quaint country rube.

As the years have gone by, this effete urban meal schedule has crept into the countryside. I once even heard the word "brunch" used in all seriousness at a local cafe! Is it any wonder our country is falling apart?

Study of history reveals that civilizations are held together by the strength and heartiness of their meals. The ancient Romans, when they were strong and virile and conquering country after country, sat down for five square meals a day, just like Minnesota Scandinavians of a generation ago.

But as the Roman Empire became decadent and began to crumble, the noon meal, once called "dinnus," was renamed "luntius." Salads crept onto their menus, mainly because the Romans were getting lazy and fat and couldn't work off a decent meal of roast beef and mashed potatoes.

In memory of their glory days, later Romans named one of their salads after Julius Caesar. But no nation which thinks of salads as a complete meal can long survive. We know what happened to the Roman Empire. We can only hope that the same fate won't befall us.

It is up to us solid folks in the countryside to preserve the old meal schedule. Keep dinner and supper at their divinely ordained hours! Ban croissants! Sit down for a sandwich at afternoon coffee! Use up the calories with hard work!

The survival of our civilization depends on it.

CHAPTER THREE

HABITS

Balancing the Checkbook

It has been about seven years since I balanced my checkbook. I can't for the life of me figure out why it is such an important duty. Isn't it enough to glance over the monthly bank statements to make sure nothing weird happened?

Yet, checkbook balancing has an aura of holiness around it, as if it were an essential ritual, a test of one's moral purity. Admitting that one doesn't balance one's checkbook is like leaving your lawn unmowed. The neighbors are going to talk.

I have three checkbooks active that I know of, all for the same account. One is in my glove compartment, another in my middle desk drawer, and the last floats from my bed stand to the top of the drier and back again.

It is nice to know that wherever I may be I will have a check nearby if I need it. If I spot a charge on my monthly statement for going under the minimum balance, I know it is time to put in some money. Phooey on this balancing business.

Remember counter checks? Those were the blank checks which each store would keep handy for their customers. Talk about convenience! I bet people who wrote counter checks weren't so careful about keeping track.

When counter checks were banned, many people were upset, just like when the phone company made us dial the prefixes on local numbers. It seemed like a plot cooked up in Moscow.

But we got used to no counter checks just like we got used to dialing seven digits to call down the road. The resilience of the human spirit is astounding.

I am afraid checks are going the way of the old party phone line. You can now pay your bills on the Internet. For purchases at the store, credit cards are just too convenient. Plus, if you use your credit card you can rack up points towards a free airline ticket.

I prefer credit cards to checks because credit cards are quicker. Nothing is worse than waiting in line at the grocery store behind somebody who not only performs the entire check writing ritual in slow motion, but insists upon balancing the checkbook before moving on. I want to yell, "The Depression is over! Hurry up before my bananas turn black!"

Unlike checks, credit cards have an air of moral depravity about them. A week doesn't go by when I don't hear some old-timer self-righteously announce that he doesn't believe in credit cards. Never has. Never will, no sir.

It is true that credit card companies are evil. They hide surprise charges in the fine print. Their offers of easy money lure the weak and the gullible. The line between Visa and Vegas is pretty thin.

Like anything, credit cards are fine as long as you are careful with them. Of course, I would never go so far as to keep track of my receipts.

Watching the Weather

The popularity of the Weather Channel must have surprised even its founders. Who would have imagined an entire channel devoted to weather 24 hours per day? And people watch it, whether they live in Florida or Alaska.

Right now, I am watching the progress of a storm on the east coast, relishing the fact that New York is getting pummeled while we are basking in sunshine. It's only eight above, yes, but sunshine is sunshine.

I used to think that only my father was interested in the weather. He had one of the first of those weather radios. He had the National Weather Service number memorized. We had indoor/outdoor thermometers all over the house long before they were available to the general public.

When the weather came on the radio, all household noise ceased. We kids froze in our tracks, no matter how rowdy our mood. It was as if Pearl Harbor had happened again. On a daily basis.

Dad would shut his eyes and go into a trancelike state, absorbing the weatherman's current prophecy, comparing it to last hour's forecast, reading between the lines, guessing which way things were moving.

I hid these facts from my peers. I thought my Dad was the only one in the world so devoted to the weather, and I did not want to be teased in school.

But I was wrong. It seems as though millions of folks in

this country consider the weather news to be the big news.

And why not? What effects us more than the weather? A slight drizzle has more effect on my day than a bombing in Israel, an economic collapse in Malaysia, or a civil war in Afghanistan.

I'll never be affected by tax cuts, budget cuts, or lying politicians enough to know the difference, but a hailstorm on my pickup is a different matter.

The Vikings may win, the Twins may lose, and the governor might shoot off his mouth, but none of those things affects me like a dust storm that fills my house with grit in May.

Yes, the weather is probably the most important news, especially when you consider that the rest of the news usually concerns celebrity divorces or other sensational but meaningless scandals.

It could be that paying attention to the weather news doesn't mean that one is boring. Instead, it might be a sign that one is busy doing things with one's life, things which inclement weather might impede.

A cousin of mine watches the Weather Channel to see if she can skydive that day. She's certainly not boring. An uncle watches to see if it is good weather for flying. He's not boring either.

As for my Dad, he watches the weather closely to make sure that the plants in the greenhouse don't freeze, or to see if he needs to hustle to get the fertilizer spread before the rain, or to finish up the fall work before the first blizzard. All pretty good reasons, it seems to me now.

Drinking Coffee

When we move back to Standard Time, life changes dramatically. With one hour of daylight lopped off the end of the day and moved to the beginning, we now find ourselves eating supper in the dark.

Coffee takes on greater importance this dark time of year, due both to its warmth and its effects as a stimulant. The main struggle of the morning is dragging oneself out to the coffee maker, dumping out yesterday's filter, and cranking up a new pot.

I am usually able to perform the coffee making ritual flawlessly, but about once per week I either forget to put water in the receptacle, which isn't much of a problem, or I forget to put the pot under the drip thing, which quickly develops into a problem.

Another trick is to leave for work without turning off the warmer under the pot. By the time I get home, the bottom of the pot is caked with sick-smelling black muck.

I am glad coffee doesn't cost all that much. I go through a pot or two every morning, although I actually drink very little. I pour it up, drink a sip, then forget about it until the cup gets cold, dump it out, refill, drink a sip, repeat until fully awake.

Coffee is an addictive drug, and I am a junkie. For me, quitting coffee means three days of headaches and many long naps. I don't even try quitting any more for fear that I will end up in the emergency room with a migraine.

Coffee may seem harmless when set against alcohol and tobacco, but too much of it can turn people into jittery wrecks. Article after article says that people who suffer from anxiety and depression should give up coffee right away.

What's more, the complicated social and psychological forces which make it so tough for people to quit drinking and smoking apply equally to coffee.

What would mornings be without the gurgle of the coffee maker? Lonely and cold. What would a trip to the local cafe be without a cup of coffee? Or a visit to an elderly friend? To turn down coffee on such occasions is like refusing communion.

Pulling a cup of hot coffee to one's lips and having the steam cloud up one's glasses makes one look thoughtful. Sipping coffee allows people to say little or nothing without seeming sullen or rude.

So, one must sometimes put one's foot down in the face of all the doom-and-gloom medical studies. Life is too short and the winters up here are too long to try to survive without the elixir which has sustained our people for generations.

Learning to Work

After a recent agonizingly slow fast-food experience, I wondered: Of all the things they teach kids in school, why don't they teach them to work?

It used to be that kids learned to work on the farm. But almost nobody farms any more. The chances of children picking up good work habits from television aren't high.

As I waited for my combo meal, I watched the three teeny boppers behind the counter flirt, giggle, push each other, and generally carry on as if I were on another planet. Finally, they shoved a tray toward me as if I had leprosy and turned back to the more important business of giggling.

When the economy booms, workers become scarce. Fast food joints are forced to dip into the middle schools to find their burger flippers. These kids clearly have more important things on their mind than customer service.

What would be wrong with teaching schoolchildren how to behave at work? It wouldn't take long.

Teenage workers should know that customers are human. All people, no matter how old and grizzled, enjoy a smile from a young face. Kindly older folks are a dime a dozen, but a personable teenager can make anybody melt.

Kids should be taught that not a dime of money goes into their pocket that didn't come out of the wallet of a customer. It is in every worker's interest to treat the customer with kindness and respect.

Teenage workers should know that skipping work doesn't mean that you are naughty and have to go to the principal. It means that you are making life miserable for your fellow workers who have to cover.

We older generations shouldn't get too self-righteous. How many of us enjoyed working in our teen years? As I recall, I hated every minute I was forced to spend away from the all-important social group.

Most of us might have benefitted from a little instruction on basic work habits at an early age. Be on time. Smile. Be attentive. Listen. Hustle.

Children should have a childhood. It is not right for a 13-year-old to be putting in long hours at a job at the same time he or she is going to school.

But if kids decide to flip burgers at the local fast food joint for a little cash, they might as well be taught to do it right. Instruction in work habits will pay off more quickly than any memorized algebra equation or lesson in frog anatomy.

Obeying the Rules

One of my many character deficiencies is my inability to keep a pocket knife. My grandfather once said, "Any nurseryman worth his salt has a pocket knife on him at all times."

I sell trees for a living, but I can't keep a pocket knife for the life of me. They disappear as fast as right-handed work gloves. So, I guess I am not worth my salt, whatever that means.

I fail to live up to many of the axioms of previous generations. For instance, if I am shoveling dirt, I don't mind taking a scoop or two from the top of the pile.

But every time I do, I remember the time our neighbor Olive caught me taking a scoop off the top of the dirt pile. She didn't just remind me that it was best to shovel from the bottom. No, she made it sound like I was guilty of a grave lapse in judgment.

Her lecture on the virtues of shoveling from the bottom of the pile included a list of the people she had seen shoveling from the top in the past. Most of them ended up serving time. As she walked away, I knew I was on her list of the doomed.

Another time, I announced to a bunch of older relatives that I didn't like to hoe weeds. Too much hard work, I said. I'd rather read.

They looked at each other as if I had just come out against the flag. Somebody mumbled, "Well, there you have it." It was obvious to them that I would never provide for myself.

Always check the oil. Always fill the tractor with gas before going out to the field. Always mow the front yard first in case the mower breaks down. Always shut the garage door so dogs don't ransack the garbage.

Shovel the steps first thing after a snow. Clean up your plate. Don't allow fresh vegetables to rot, even if you have bushels extra. Can them. Freeze them. But don't let them go to waste.

Don't waste a stamp, even if it means driving ten miles to pay a bill. Save the wax paper from cereal boxes. Use gift wrap over and over until it goes limp. Recycle aluminum foil until it is caked with blackened roast drippings.

These rules are ingrained in me, even though I break them daily. When I toss out a cottage cheese container instead of saving it for leftovers, I can see long-dead neighbors and relatives shaking their heads in dismay.

What would they think if they knew I frequently run my pocket knife through the wash? Doesn't he clean out his pockets, they'd say. You'd think he'd take care of his things. Knives aren't cheap. Kids these days don't know what hard times are!

Taking Naps

The world is divided into two opposing and hostile factions: Those who nap, and those who do not.

Nappers appreciate the sacred and holy importance of napping. As members of the Order of the Nap, they know that upon entering a house, any house, at any time of day, a decent person will act as if somebody is trying to nap until he finds out otherwise.

Non-nappers slam doors, stomp on stairs, talk boisterously, and bang kettles even when they know very well somebody is trying to sleep. They view it as their duty to destroy naps, as if by rousing the nappers they are helping the economy.

Many nappers struggle with shame over their enjoyment of naps. They apologize for snoozing, as if they have violated some sacred principle by dozing off during the day.

Such shame is unjustified and wrong. In fact, nappers are a superior breed. Nappers have a greater perspective. They realize that perpetual busyness and running in circles is not all there is to life.

Napper support groups are helping to change society's view of nappers. More and more, nappers everywhere are rising up to assert their rights.

Those rights include the right to be undisturbed by telemarketers. There should be a constitutional amendment to limit the free speech of telemarketers, perhaps suppress it altogether. Those jerks ruin countless naps. They should be completely stifled.

Non-nappers should be forced to attend sensitivity training workshops on napping in order to better understand the rights and needs of nappers.

Non-nappers also should be trained in the latest methods of noise suppression. They should learn how to walk down stairs without tromping like an elephant, how to get breakfast ready without making the kitchen sound like a machine shop, and how to turn off those beepers on large equipment.

Meanwhile, nappers must continue to educate society about nappers and napping. Nappers in prominent positions should come forward publicly so young nappers have adequate role models from an early age.

I was fortunate to grow up in a family where napping was tolerated and honored. If somebody was napping, our home was as quiet as a morgue. The stereo was equipped with head-phones, and the piano had a soft pedal.

But when I went forth into the world, I was forced to live in a dormitory where napping was not appreciated or under-stood. What a cruel shock. Naphood became difficult to attain, and my morale sank.

Now I live alone in the middle of nowhere. My nap life is healthy and fulfilling. Sometimes I have one of those naps where you wake up and don't know where you are, what century it is, or whether it is morning or evening. Ah, nirvana!

But we cannot forget the millions who are not so lucky, those who suffer silently in a noisy world hostile to napping.

Stealing Fruit

Fresh strawberries! Is there anything better?

I am typing with red-stained fingers after my most recent trip to the berry patch. I never return from the patch with any berries, I just eat them on the spot.

Fresh, home-grown strawberries are far superior to the stuff you get in the store. Store-bought berries have white, foamy middles, but home-grown berries are juicy red all the way through. Store-bought berries are firm and tough, but home-grown berries melt in your mouth.

Store-bought berries have a watery flavor, but home-grown ones, especially those breeds which are on the verge of being a wild strawberry, have flavor that won't quit.

Store-bought strawberries, even at their very best, are likely to deserve no more than a "not bad" rating. But when I crush one of those home-grown berries in my mouth, them flavor juices flow and I see rainbows, fireworks, and hear a symphony orchestra. It's quite something.

I once ate too many fresh strawberries. I broke out into hives and itched like crazy. I am surprised they didn't warn us against eating too many berries in Sunday School or in health class. There is always a price to pay for having too much fun!

I still feel vaguely guilty when I sneak out to the strawberry batch to gorge myself for ten minutes. I make sure nobody is watching. I try to avoid incriminating stains on my knees or my fingers.

But I am not the only one. When the strawberries ripen, you can often catch people who are supposed to be cultivating or mowing take a detour past the strawberry patch. They'll look around to make sure nobody is looking, leave the tractor at a high idle to make it sound like they are working, and dig in.

Once in the patch, they get carried away. The tractor idles and idles while they fill themselves up with berries, glancing around every now and then to see if the coast is clear.

Forbidden fruit tastes better than anything you buy in the store. The more forbidden the fruit, the better the flavor.

Crabapples taste far better out of the neighbor's tree. If the neighbor is a cranky, card carrying member of the NRA, the flavor of the pilfered apples can be unbeatable.

Is there anything better than asparagus harvested out of a county ditch five miles south? Such slyly obtained asparagus is much better than store-bought asparagus, and much better than asparagus harvested from one's own garden.

Yes, the best fruit in the world is harvested in the wild, off of somebody else's land, with a hint of danger, and a sense that one is getting away with something a little naughty.

Stopping to Help

The other night, I was confronted with one of life's great moral quandaries. The driver of a stalled car attempted to flag me down on the highway. What does one do, drive coldly past, forget about the stranded people a mile later, and go home to a blissful night's sleep? Or, stop to help and and get mixed up in the problems of somebody one has never met?

I figured that on the off chance that the stranded motorists were ax murderers, at least my obituary would read nicely: "He died as he lived, helping others."

So, with the purest of motives, I stopped to see what the trouble was.

They had burnt up their engine. They had been meaning to check the oil, but hadn't gotten around to it. They had just been to a class reunion. They weren't from the area. They seemed to have enjoyed themselves a great deal at the class reunion.

They did not have roadside assistance. They had no money. They had no phone card. They had no relatives. And for some reason or another, they didn't seem interested in receiving assistance from law enforcement.

I was tempted to lecture them on the virtues of regularly scheduled maintenance and the value of getting home at a decent hour in a decent condition. I was also tempted to jump in my pickup and head home to bed.

But, I thought, who am I to judge? There but for the grace

of God go I. Who knows, my life could at any time spiral downwards, even to the point where I would stop checking my oil. Yes, even I could one day find myself stranded late at night in the middle of nowhere with no real excuse.

So I drove the woman to the nearest town. We found a phone booth. Using my phone card, she called a friend 100 miles away. It was the only number she could remember.

The woman's friend had many questions about why this happened and why so late at night and why suddenly now do you call after I haven't talked to you in nine months and just what am I supposed to do about it, and so on.

The phone call consumed much of my pre-paid phone card. But it was a success. Enticed by a generous offer of cash, the groggy friend agreed to make the 100 mile trip.

I don't know where the cash was going to come from, because the woman told me she was utterly broke. She half-heartedly offered to dig in her seat cushions for some change to pay for the phone call, but I told her not to bother.

Actually, the overpowering feeling of self-righteousness I got from helping a stranger in trouble was all the compensation I needed. Plus, think of all of the mileage I can get out of the story about the idiots who didn't get around to checking their oil!

Curing Boredom

It occurred to me the other day that I have never heard a person over the age of forty use the phrase, "I'm bored." It is a complaint reserved solely for the young.

Of course, it is always proper to say that you find another person boring. That's just telling the truth. The world is full of boring people. But watching them, studying them, and figuring them out is anything but boring.

The person who says "I'm bored," is saying a lot about themselves. They expect somebody to entertain them at all times. When they aren't taken care of in such a manner, they say "I am bored," which is the equivalent of a baby crying for a bottle.

Whenever I am tempted to say, "I'm bored," I think of people who spent years in solitary confinement in a prison camp during the war, or of the hostages in Iran twenty years ago. If anybody had an excuse to complain of boredom, it was them.

Yet, the prisoners who came through with their sanity found ways to turn the long days into something useful. They found that they could remember hymns, poems and books from their youth. They wrote songs in their heads. They developed methods of communicating with other prisoners by tapping, or by passing tiny notes.

I think about hostages every time I am stuck waiting in a doctor's office with a ragged four-year-old copy of *People* magazine. At least I have a chair, some people to watch, and a magazine to study for its absurdities. Things could be worse.

Every now and then, I begin to resent the quiet of country living and start wishing for some city bustle. I repeat the teenager's lament: "There's nothing to do." I long for an Asian restaurant within walking distance, or perhaps a good used book store.

Well, I have a house full of books, a stereo, a piano to play, and this blame computer to write on. There is no excuse for boredom in such a situation! I am beginning to think that to a mature adult there is never a legitimate reason to say, "I'm bored."

Even when caught in your car at a railroad crossing waiting for an endless coal train to pass, or while waiting for a delayed plane at the airport, or when stuck at an obligatory party where nobody seems interesting, even in those awful situations there is no real excuse to say, "I'm bored."

The most boring party can be made interesting by studying the titles of the books on the shelves of the host, or by asking strange, off-the-wall questions of the boring people. So, Mrs. Johnson, have you ever let your hair out of its bun? Wore slacks? Skipped church? Drank too much?

As for the trains, have you ever tried to figure out the graffiti on the rail cars and wondered where those cars had been before they were sent across the prairie? They weren't sitting in North Dakota, I can tell you that much.

Taking Pills

Whatever pollen it is that attacks my nasal passages every August decided to strike last evening at nine o'clock. Fellow hay feverites are familiar with the tickling in the mouth, the violent sneezing, the draining nose, the itchy eyes.

As a card carrying hypochondriac, I have my cupboard stocked with over-the-counter medicines of every sort. Vitamin C, vitamin E, vitamin A, echinacea, Sudafed, kelp, calcium, bee pollen, garlic, alfalfa tablets, melatonin, the works. And those are just the legal ones.

I dug through all of that stuff last night, but I didn't have a single night-time allergy pill to help me get some sleep. No, all I had were those "non-drowsy" cold pills, known as "speed" in college circles.

Take two non-drowsy pills at bedtime and you will spend the night cleaning house, washing dishes, pounding on the piano, or calling relatives in California. By morning, you will have vowed to learn a foreign language, write a book, tell off your boss, and clean the garage.

Your ambition will last until breakfast when you will collapse in a heap and sleep all day. Your sleep schedule will be screwed up for weeks.

So, the non-drowsy pills were out, and I was stuck thirty-four miles from the nearest all-night convenience store. Suddenly the solitude and quiet of country living didn't seem so wonderful.

I decided to tough it out. I would use my mental powers to overcome the sneeze impulse. I sat in my recliner and chanted, "My nose does not itch, my nose does not itch." I imagined myself breathing freely on a Pacific island.

The power of positive thinking works on television, but it didn't do much for me. When I started another round of sneezing, I felt spiritually deficient, not up to those people on TV who are so easily able to heal and get healed.

As a last resort, I worked my way through the pill bottle collection and swallowed one of each thing, hoping one of them would work on my allergies. I even took some ginseng, just in case. After a five minute break, I threw back a couple more Vitamin C for good measure. Nothing worked. Eventually, my over-the-counter drug binge caused me to pass out on the recliner and have the worst dreams I have had in months. Have you ever gotten stuck at the top of a wobbly ferris wheel without clothes on? After last night, I can say that I have.

First thing in the morning, I bought some good antihistamines. I swallowed them without water and stayed in the air conditioned drug store for a half-hour until they took effect. As the chemicals began to flow through my veins, a feeling of calm and well-being crept over me.

Until frost kills the pollen, I will be utterly dependent upon drugs for my happiness. Betty Ford might not approve, but I don't mind a bit.

Exercising

Its one thing to be physically fit, but is another to torture one's body in hopes that physical misery is going to make one live longer or better.

I was in Duluth a couple of weekends ago when they held their annual marathon. I didn't see the race, but the next day I saw people of all ages limping around town. They didn't look healthy at all.

That next evening, I took a walk around downtown Duluth. The weather was cool and sunny. The birds chirped. The scent of lilacs filled the air. Lake Superior was blue and dotted with sailboats. It was a wonderful evening for a walk.

I wondered where all the people were, until I passed a health club. Through the enormous front window, I saw about a dozen people on treadmills, sweating to beat the band. Some wore earphones. Others watched a TV hanging from the wall. All of them looked miserable.

I thought, are these people insane? It was probably one of the most beautiful evenings of the year. Duluth is full of sidewalks and walking trails, yet these people chose to walk on a plastic belt in some smelly health club.

It occurred to me: Can you imagine a field mouse stupid enough to jump into a stinky cage just so he could run on the little wire wheel for an hour? I doubt it. Yet, it was no problem to find a dozen human beings, allegedly the most intelligent animals on the earth, willing to come in from the beautiful outdoors to trudge along on a treadmill, and pay for the privilege!

People seem to think that to be healthy one has to torment one's self with tasteless food and grueling exercise. "No pain, no gain," goes the saying.

But what good does intense exercise do for such people? Do these self-tormenters ever slow down to enjoy life?

Even when the exercise puritans do their thing outside, they refuse to enjoy themselves. The birds chirp, yet they wear headphones. The scenery is beautiful, yet they stare straight ahead. A walk might be enjoyed and savored, yet they make sure it is miserable by carrying a weight in each hand and flailing their arms in an exaggerated manner.

In the old days, people called a walk a "constitutional," implying that the purpose of the activity wasn't just to get one's heart pumping. The fresh air, the birds, the time away from daily hassles, and the refreshment of the soul was as much a part of exercise as was the moving of the legs.

Now, however, people seem determined to make exercise just another part of the rat race. They apparently hope their heroic efforts will earn them a few extra months before their fatal heart attack. Then, finally, they will relax!

Controlling Fate

Just so we don't forget the Great Depression, most every spring treats us to a week of hot, dry winds which fills houses, ears and noses with a fine grit. The winds are needed to dry the fields, but the dust we could do without.

What is it about wind that completely tires one out? Even while sitting inside, hearing the wind rattle the windows and roar through the trees makes one want to nap.

"Yep, it sure is late this year," is spring's small-talk catch phrase. Every spring seems to be late. Since I started caring about these things, I recall one early spring and nineteen late ones. Perhaps our standards are too high.

The Great First Tomato Competition is starting in earnest. Nobody crowns a winner or gives a prize, but it is still important to some people to have the first ripe tomato in the tri-state area.

It's mostly the men, of course, who turn everything into a competition. They plant just after the snow melts, and then build fortresses around their tomato plants to protect them from the last blizzard.

Three weeks after that first tomato, there are so many tomatoes in the country that you can't give them away. By the end of August, tomatoes rot by the millions in gardens all across the area.

But in May, the thought of biting into that first ripe tomato inspires gardeners to go to great lengths.

Potatoes are supposed to be planted on Good Friday, according to some folk proverb, which this year meant planting them in the snow banks.

Old wives' and old husbands' tales abound in the realm of vegetable gardening. Some plant on the new moon, some plant on the full moon, others plant at midnight.

Everybody has their own superstitions. Vegetables are so easy to grow that it isn't difficult to conclude that whatever hocus pocus one performed works. If a person happens to plant beans the day of Luther League one year and gets a good crop, they'll do the same for the next forty.

My superstitions relate to baseball. I believe I have power over the Minnesota Twins. If I tune into the middle of a game and the opposing team is batting, I change the station right away before something bad happens. If the Twins are batting, then I am free to listen.

If the Twins only realized how much they depended up me to do the right things, eat the right meals before game time, listen to the broadcast from the right chair, or change the station to put a stop to an opponent's big inning, they would pay somebody to keep track of me.

People with garden superstitions have it better. At least they can weed, water and fertilize to help make their superstitions seem true.

Faking Friendliness

It is time to ban artificial, manufactured, trained, forced, corporate cheerfulness!

I just called a hotel, and instead of hearing the usual, "Hello, Dixie's Deluxe Hotel," I was treated to the following lingo: "You're someone special at Dixie's Deluxe Hotel, this is Trevor, how can I help you?"

I couldn't hold back. I blurted out, "You poor kid, having to answer the phone like that!" Trevor stuttered around before connecting me to the room I wished to call.

Ten minutes later, I called again, half trying to get ahold of a friend at the hotel, and half trying to see if these people were for real.

They were. Once again: "You're someone special at Dixie's Deluxe Hotel, this is Amanda, how can I help you?"

"Well, you're special too, Amanda," I said. "Please connect me to room 241."

This phony friendliness is spreading like an epidemic throughout American business.

You go to a chain restaurant, and the wait-persons act as if they are reading off of cue cards. "Hi, my name is Mindy, and I will be your server tonight."

"Well, my name is Eric, and I am going to be your customer tonight," I sometimes reply with a toothy, fake grin.

But that is rude. None of this is Mindy's fault. It is the fault of some idiot back at headquarters who decided that you can stuff people's head with memorized phrases which will make them seem helpful even when they really don't care.

Chain restaurant wait-persons are trained to come back to the table every five minutes, clasp their hands, smile, and say, "Is there anything else I can get you folks tonight?"

I beat one waitress to the punch. As she approached for her obligatory visit, I asked for some ketchup.

She acted annoyed and mumbled okay. Then, despite already knowing what I wanted, she clasped her hands, pasted on a plastic grin and said in a sing-songy voice, "Is there anything else that I can get you folks tonight?"

I had already told her what else I needed that night, and it was ketchup, but she stuck to her script. The ketchup never came.

What would be wrong with training servicepersons to treat others like they would like others to treat them? Service can't be memorized or faked. It has to come from the heart.

The bogus "You're someone special..." lingo at Dixie's Deluxe does the hotel no good. It just makes me cranky. I don't want some Trevor or Amanda telling me that I am special. Trevor and Amanda don't know me, and they probably wouldn't think I was special if they did.

Deciding

Life's smallest decisions can be the toughest. Over my lifetime, I have spent hours in front of vending machines deciding which button to push, as if my happiness depended upon choosing an Almond Joy over a Snickers.

I love Chinese food, but it drives me nuts to have to choose from 213 items on the menu, none of which I understand. The poor waitress has to come back four times before I am finally ready to make up my mind. In the end, I always get the Moo Shu pork because I have had it before, and I am too lazy to try something new.

With soda pop, I have solved the dilemma of choice by sticking with Coke, not because it is superior, but because I am too lazy to reconsider my beverage preference each day.

Such laziness is the basis of most habits. We buy Buicks for forty years running because we know the dealer and it is easier just to go back to the same place. We go to the same grocery store because we know where to find the milk and the bread without having to ask or think.

Habits are helpful as long as we realize that they are little more than a way to make life easier by cutting down on the number of decisions one must make every day.

But inevitably we take our habits one step farther and insist that our preferences are good, right and true. Coke drinkers began to think they are superior to Pepsi drinkers. Buick drivers become convinced that Buicks are actually the best vehicle.

We see habits in others as being noble, even if those habits differ from ours. "He always bought John Deeres," the neighbors say with admiration at a neighbor's funeral, as if switching from brand to brand would have been a form of promiscuity.

In the same way people stick with the same political and religious ideas for years and years, not so much because they are convinced that they have found the truth, but because they don't want to go through the pain of thinking about those things all over again.

Nothing causes the mind more pain than having to change one's ideas. Thinking causes wrinkles and ulcers. We fight at every turn to keep our old ideas.

But, mindless habit isn't always bad. It speeds up the lines at the vending machines, for one thing.

CHAPTER FOUR

GROWING OLD

Old Neighbors

On Memorial Day, I think of neighbors. Most of the neighbors around the farm where I grew up are gone. Their children
moved away, their farmsteads were bulldozed, and the marker
in the cemetery is all that is left of them.

The old neighbors had neighborly rituals, and with them,
those rituals died.

Neighbors Lewis and Mable Nelson picked blueberries over
by Bemidji every summer. A few weeks later, Mable would host
a big meal for the neighbors, topped off by blueberry pie. It
was an annual event.

Neighbor Henry Helm was a wiry old German who walked
in big long strides and smoked Salems. His forearms were like
Popeye's, but the rest of him was barely there.

I was scared to death of Henry. He trapped on our land,
but I never once saw him in our woods—only his widely-spaced
footsteps. He wasn't much for children and when I was small
I wondered if he trapped them too.

But Henry had an old Beacon apple tree which bore the
sweetest, reddest apples you have ever seen. Every year, Henry
would bring over a bag full. We had apples galore on our own
place, but none like Henry's Beacon apples. When he brought
them over I realized that he wasn't so scary after all.

By fifth grade I even mustered the courage to ask Henry
if I could watch the first game of the 1975 World Series on his
color TV. Henry fixed Kool-aid, and the Red Sox won behind

legendary Cuban pitcher Luis Tiant.

In 1977, Lewis and Mable Nelson went blueberry picking on July 4th as always. They picked as much as usual, but this time it was too much for Mable's heart—she passed away that evening, before she could make any of her famous blueberry pie.

Sadly, no fall meal at the Nelson's. But that October, Grandpa called up Lewis to see if we could watch the sixth game of the World Series on Lewis' color TV.

Lewis made us hot chocolate. Reggie Jackson hit three home runs on three consecutive pitches. And it was the last time I was in the Nelson house before Lewis moved to town.

The next winter as I was about to get off the school bus one cold evening, Art the bus driver said, "So, you lost a neighbor." Henry Helm had died suddenly that morning. I thought right away of that World Series game, the only time I ever spent with Henry.

When summer came, somebody went over to sneak some of the famous apples off of Henry's tree. No luck. Henry's Beacon apple tree was stone dead. It hadn't survived the winter either.

So, most of the old neighbors are gone, some precious rituals have disappeared, but many good memories remain: Blueberries and Beacon apples, grand old neighbors, and some great ball games.

Sharp as Tacks

One group of people intrigues me more than any other: People well into their nineties who still have all their marbles.

Harold Stassen died last week at age ninety-three. He was active to the end, still thinking about public policy.

Also last week, I attended the funeral of a ninety-six year old local man, Art Rongen. Art baked, cooked, gardened and helped with the farm up to his last few days. He was featured in a recent book, "Haymakers."

At lunch after the funeral, I visited with a ninety-six year old woman who plans to fly to Florida next week for a little vacation. The winters get long, you know.

Earlier in the week, I stopped at the nursing home and had a good chat with two ninety-seven year olds. Both were as sharp as tacks. They had been classmates in country school ninety years ago. I asked one of them who was the first president she remembered, and she shot back, "Lincoln, I suppose!"

Good grief, what makes these people tick? If you ask them the secret to their longevity and good health, most are too crafty to give a straight answer.

Some attribute their long life to no booze, others swear by a snort of brandy every night. The Queen Mother of England, soon to be 101, reportedly downs a pint of gin per day.

Some didn't smoke, others did. Some ate a lot of yogurt, others fried bacon and eggs every morning. My jolly old neigh bor Fred Brown ate at least one slice of pie every day, and it showed. He lived to age 96.

It seems that health habits are less important to a long life than attitude. What many very old people have in common, in my mind, is an unusual ability to recover from life's difficulties and a steadfast refusal to dwell in self pity.

It never bothered Harold Stassen that he lost his last few dozen elections despite his brilliant public service career early in life. He had every excuse to be bitter, resentful and self-pitying, but those thoughts never seem to have crossed his mind.

I once read an interview with a 112-year old woman. She had just learned that morning that her eighty-five year old daughter had died of old age, yet she insisted that the interview go forward. You feel sad, she said, but you have to move on.

You don't find these people paying much attention to fiber and cholesterol and exercise and vitamins. In fact, most people in their nineties rightly feel they have earned the right to ignore that stuff all together.

But these grand old men and women all seem to share a particular attitude. They are determined to enjoy what they have while they have it. They respond to life's blows by pulling themselves together and moving forward.

In fact, they seem to regard self-pity to be a type of cancer as fatal as any other.

An Old Teacher's Advice

I ran into one of my favorite elementary school teachers, Mrs. Corrine Hermanson, at an all-school reunion 10 years ago. She was an excellent teacher, a stern taskmaster from the old school.

In the third grade, I was Mrs. Hermanson's pet. That meant that when she threw her used tissues in the general direction of the waste basket and missed, I had to pick them up.

At the reunion, Mrs. Hermanson appeared out of the blue as we gathered for our class photo. She was in her eighties by that time, but didn't look much different than she had 20 years before. She still smelled of cigarette smoke and exotic perfumes.

I greeted her warmly, but true to form, Mrs. Hermanson just stuck her crooked finger in my chest and growled, "Never, never, never retire. Retirement is not good." With that last little lesson, she greeted a few others, and walked out. I never saw her again.

I think Mrs. Hermanson was right. What is the point of retirement, anyway? It is crazy that people spend their lives working their tails off at jobs they hate so they can retire. And, if you enjoy your work, why quit?

When people quit work, what do they do? Many die right away. Others become depressed. Some are too tired and decrepit to enjoy the retirement for which they have worked so hard and long.

Fortunately, most people simply switch work. "I am busier than I have ever been," they say, which is a sign that they have adjusted just fine to retirement and aren't idle.

No, the trick is to find work you love and do it until you drop. I admire people like Ed, a neighbor who died while milking cows at age 86.

Or Geneva, the legendary restaurant hostess in Fargo who is approaching 90, yet still shows up for work in her glamorous hats to seat the customers with style.

Or Rose Blumkin, the Omaha furniture store owner who, despite being a millionaire many times over, managed a furniture store until her death at age 104.

It isn't good to see physically healthy people become entirely idle. Full-time retired folks often lose their sense of self-worth. They have surrendered that which gave them significance.

Often people who retire have no choice. Business and government policies force many people to retire cold turkey.

Wouldn't it be better if people could simply taper off as they get older? Think of the accumulated wisdom companies lose by throwing away older people as if they are worthless.

It seems that one key to a long, happy life is to keep busy at work one loves for as long as one can keep going. But that's easier said than done. What a rare privilege it has become to die with one's boots on!

Facing Winter

The first acorns to fall in late August are a signal that summer is nearing its end. Soon the maples in lake country will show their first signs of orange.

The early signs of autumn always give me a jolt. Seems like we just got rid of the snow and already my survival instincts are urging me to build up the woodpile again.

One can be a pessimist and groan that the days are getting shorter, and that it is all downhill from here. Or, one can be an optimist and enjoy the brilliant days of late summer and autumn. Is there any more beautiful time of year?

Reminds me of when I first realized my hair was getting thin. I was age twenty-three. That discovery was a jolt, terrifying evidence that my body was starting its long downhill slide. Thinning hair, expanding gut, blurring eyesight—could bypass surgery be far behind?

I ran out and picked up some of that hair fertilizer stuff, hoping to forestall the inevitable. I irrigated my scalp faithfully and searched my head for signs of new growth.

That project lasted a couple of weeks before I decided that putting off aging is about as futile as trying to postpone winter. I decided to take good care of what I have and leave it at that.

Part of the secret of aging gracefully, it seems, is not to try to cover up the fact that you are growing older. For instance, instead of being boldly bald, many men coil long strands of their remaining hair on top of their bald spot. Some women get face lifts which stretch their skin as tightly as Saran Wrap on a bowl of leftovers.

But age has advantages beyond senior discounts at Hardee's. The older people I most admire have used their years to gain a sense of peace and calm. They have adjusted. They look comfortable in their wrinkled skin. Years of experience have made them wise.

According to the insurance charts, I am less than half way to the grave. But even if my life is half over, I would not go back to being ten years younger if I were paid. Can you think of anybody in their twenties who has their act together, who is calm and serene? I may not be all together now, but I was worse off then.

It is understandable that we usually don't see the benefits of getting older. But one had just as well enjoy the fruits of the ripening days rather than fight the inevitable decline and become bitter. Either way, winter is going to come.

Obituaries

The first thing I look for in the paper in the morning is the obituary section. Younger people might think this habit morbid, but if you live for any length of time in the northern Minnesota countryside, you not only come to know hundreds of people, but you eventually realize that most of them are over seventy years old. The "Area Deaths" column is a place to catch up with friends and neighbors.

Even obituaries of people I don't know fascinate me simply for the history they contain. Each obituary contains a brief story of one life. Oscar fought at Normandy. Joanne worked in an airplane factory on the coast during the war. Ingevald came with his parents from Norway in 1910.

In the obituaries are bits and pieces of our nation's past. Immigration. Wars. The Depression. The older the deceased, the more interesting the story. I haven't seen the obituary of a World War I veteran for some time, but references to World War II are still frequent.

Some obituaries are so sketchy that readers are forced to read between the lines to figure out the truth.

For example, an obituary might read, "In 1956, the deceased was united in marriage to Ed Jones. Together, they bore three children. In 1965, she was married to Bill Johnson. They moved to Mesa, AZ in 1985. He died in 1989."

Wait a minute here, what happened to old Ed? Is he dead or alive? Did the deceased decide to add another husband on a whim? Did Ed go along to Arizona? If you are going to bring up Ed in the first place, don't just leave him hanging!

There was a divorce in there somewhere, of course. Or Ed just ran off. But nobody wants that stuff mentioned in their obituary.

I suspect the truth suffers even more in some of those newfangled death notices where the family can say whatever they want. Many of the people featured in those paid notices seem qualified for sainthood.

It could be that the survivors are doing a little posthumous lobbying on behalf of the deceased, or maybe these people truly did have a "deep and abiding faith." We'll never know, and I guess it is none of our business.

After all, most obituaries contain some fiction, if only because we strive to make life seem orderly when it is seldom anything of the sort.

A truthful obituary of myself right now would say something like: He wandered through college with no real purpose and never used his degree. He finally came back and took over the family business because he was too stubborn to work for anybody else.

But I won't presume to write my own obituary. That's not my job. If some future obituary writer wants to dress up the truth a little bit, more power to them.

Baseball and Grandpa

With spring comes the beginning of the baseball season. As a child, I could barely wait for Opening Day. Every spring I was convinced that this was the year the Twins would win it all.

My grandfather introduced me to baseball in 1974. I was in third grade. He would lie on the couch in the old house with the ball game blaring at full volume. How Grandma put up with it is anybody's guess.

During the mid-seventies, the Twins struggled. That didn't prevent Grandpa and me from spending the late winter evenings debating every shred of Twins news. When the baseball gurus predicted that the Twins would finish last, we agreed that they were part of a vast anti-Minnesota conspiracy.

A couple of years later Grandpa subscribed to the Minneapolis Tribune so we could read Sid Hartman. Sid, an eternal optimist, would fuel our belief that the Twins were just a player or two away from winning the World Series.

We sat for hours in the old house listening to Herb Carneal do the play-by-play. Grandpa, a militant teetotaler, would turn off the radio during the beer commercials.

We listened until the Twins pitchers gave up home runs in bunches. Then Grandpa would jump out of his recliner in disgust and storm outside to pull weeds, even at dusk. If a Twins hitter took a called third strike with the bases loaded, Grandpa would need to pop a nitroglycerin pill.

Then came the late eighties, a few winning Twins teams, and easy access to televised baseball. By then, Grandpa was in the nursing home. You would think that baseball would have provided him with the ideal pastime.

Not at all. Televised baseball annoyed Grandpa. Too many beer ads. All of those players drooling tobacco juice. Plus, Grandpa couldn't stand how Tom Kelly let his glasses slide down on the end of his nose.

Baseball on the radio wasn't what it used to be, either. Halsey Hall was dead. Herb Carneal was doing fewer innings, and his sidekick John Gordon had an announcing style comparable to fingernails on a chalkboard.

Grandpa sat in his recliner with his remote control in one hand so he could shut the television off during beer ads and shots of Tom Kelly in the dugout. His other hand controlled the volume knob of the radio so he could tune out John Gordon.

It sometimes got to be too much work, especially when Hrbek would take a third strike with the bases loaded. Grandpa would then shut off all the gadgets, and lay in bed and fume.

When the Twins won the World Series in 1987, Grandpa didn't watch much of it. Too hard on his heart. In fact, I think he was happier when the Twins were a losing team and he could go take out his frustrations with them on the weeds!

Fido at Fair Meadow

On a recent trip to a nursing home, I was startled when a furball scurried past my feet. I thought a squirrel had snuck in the door, but it was a cat. I soon discovered there was also a puppy in the building. Both animals were permanent residents.

What a great idea! I snooped a little and found that many area nursing homes have pets running loose. "Companion animals," as they are called in the official parlance, have become a trend in nursing home care.

I asked residents at the local home what they thought of the animals. It was clear that they enjoyed them thoroughly. Only one woman complained, but she complains about everything. Having something more to complain about probably makes her happy, too.

Now, why didn't this happen thirty years ago? I remember how thrilled nursing home residents were when they first put in fish tanks and bird cages, and fish and birds aren't nearly as much fun as cats and puppies.

A nursing home is a great place for animals. Is there anywhere cats and dogs could give and get more love? Think of all the people who leave their dogs home alone in an apartment all day while they work. No such lonely times for a pet in a nursing home. I am sure there are plenty of table scraps, too.

During my visit, the resident cat jumped up onto the lap

of Nora, who is in a wheelchair. Nora hasn't been able to speak since her stroke, but she smiled from ear to ear when the cat snuggled up to her.

I didn't meet the puppy. He was busy running in and out of rooms down on the other wing. I'll bet there were smiles all around.

The older I get, the more I enjoy animals. They aren't as complicated as people. They give unconditional love. They don't care if your hair is messy or if your clothes were purchased ten years ago. They are content with the same food every day.

Even the crankiest older people—those who have grown weary of other humans and have put up a wall of crabbiness to keep other people out of their hair—even those people melt in the presence of a friendly animal.

My grandma would moan and groan every time a stray cat showed up on her step. Time to get the gun, she would say. We don't want that scruffy-looking varmint around here.

Ten minutes later, she would be heating milk on the stove.

It is good that some animals can live in nursing homes where their affection is appreciated most. Humans are fine, but when I get eighty-five and a little cranky, the company of a cat will probably be a good thing.

CHAPTER FIVE

CHANGES

There Went the Neighborhood

The present farm crisis gets a lot of attention, but farms have disappeared at a steady pace for the past 30 years.

In my township of Bear Park, the voting rolls have declined from 300 to about 110 just in my short memory. Several country churches have closed, and a majority of the farmsteads have been bulldozed and turned into fields.

The Bear Park Store, a little country store in the middle of nowhere, closed in the mid-nineties.

It makes me sad to think of all of the old oak trees which only recently grew on land which now produces a few bushels of nearly worthless wheat.

I often drive past an open field that used to be the farmstead of my dear old neighbors, Mildred and Elmer.

What a wonderful place they had! A row of lilacs surrounded their deep, dark woods. Tucked in the clearing deep in the grove sat their old house, along with an orchard and some sway-backed out buildings.

Each apple tree in their orchard had a story. Elmer told me many times of the tree an uncle of mine had given Elmer's son for graduation. It bore buckets of delicious apples every year.

Elmer and Mildred had long since retired from farming by the time I knew them, but their farmstead still had rustic charm. The decrepit granary was full of pigeons. Elmer did woodwork in his ramshackle shop.

Their garden was plentiful, and Mildred's kitchen brimmed with old-fashioned smells of baking, canning and good cooking. I often rode my bike over to their place just for the adventure.

As Mildred and Elmer grew older, I frequently mowed their lawn. The yard was full of little hills and vallies, nooks and crannies, peonies, old-fashioned roses and moss-covered tree stumps. I mowed it all in exchange for a good meal of meat loaf or fried chicken.

But the cruel rules of economics wiped out the whole works. When Elmer and Mildred moved away, the high wheat prices of that time made it inevitable that the next land owner would bulldoze the woods, the old house, and the granary to plant crops.

Elmer and Mildred died soon after they left the farm. Their children disappeared into the city to find jobs and haven't been heard from since.

Few people who drive by that open grain field today have any idea how many wonderful times were had on that little patch of land.

The many changes are probably inevitable. There is no stopping progress.

But when the apple trees and lilacs are in full bloom, I think back to Mildred and Elmer, their cozy farm yard, the good meals, and I get a little sad.

Burning The Garbage

It is illegal to burn one's garbage nowadays. Every farm is supposed to have a dumpster and recycle bins. You are now obligated by law to hire big trucks to come and get your junk.

Yet, I see neighbors burning fields, stacks of old hay and straw, grub piles and leaf piles. None of them end up in jail. I stuff my old cereal boxes and milk cartons in the wood stove and torch them. Is that any better than burning garbage outside in a rusty fifty gallon drum?

A few years back, the ever-meddlesome Minnesota legislature decided that it should be illegal to throw away old phone books. You are supposed to recycle them. I suspect that law was designed for the cities, where each phone book consumes half a tree.

Just to spite the bureaucrats and do-gooders in the legislature, I burned my little phone book in my wood stove last fall. I felt no guilt. Nothing has happened to me yet, and the statute of limitations will run out soon enough.

When I was a kid, Dad dug a pit out back for garbage. We would pile it up with junk of all sorts. When the pit got full, I'd ask my father if I could burn the dump. He would check the wind and say go ahead.

Soon after I lit it, the fire would take off. I pretended that the garbage pile was a little city burning to the ground. When the cardboard boxes dissolved in flames, I imagined they were skyscrapers.

As the fire grew hot, the pit fizzed and squealed. Aerosol cans and fluorescent bulbs exploded like bombs bursting in air. When plastics caught fire, big billows of dense black smoke belched upwards, and strands of black ash wafted down. Those were the days!

We had the most fun when one of the many old sheds on the farm needed to go. The men would push the building into a big pile. It was understood that the wreckage would just sit there until my uncle came home from the cities. The night he arrived, Dad and he would wait until it was dark, dowse the pile with fuel oil, and torch the whole works.

What an event! Flames roared upwards. The fire singed the leaves on trees up to fifty yards away. You could feel the heat on the front step of the house.

There was a sense that burning was a very important task, a dangerous job big men took very seriously. Of course now I realize that the men were just being little boys. They were having as much fun as I did when I burned the garbage pit.

The state is right. We shouldn't pollute. We should recycle. We should use our dumpsters.

Even so, do the do-good bureaucrats realize that their regulations rob countless boys ages eight to eighty of the traditional joys of a big fire?

Goodbye Rural Route 1

I used to live on Rural Route 1. Now, thanks to the new 911 address system, I live at 10345 125th Street West, or something like that.

One of my older friends was amused by her new address. "I've lived in this same swamp for 53 years," she said, "and now they are calling it Main Street West!"

The first of these crazy new addresses I ever saw was 187th St. SW in Buxton, ND. I was sure some impish North Dakota person invented the impressive-sounding address to get more respect when ordering stuff over the phone from New York.

Then I got notice of my new address. No more rural route. The cow path past my place had been transformed into 125th Street West.

The idea behind these complicated addresses is that the ambulances and fire crews will be able to find remote farmsteads more easily. To check that theory out, I called the 911 people to see where they would end up if I had an emergency and was unable to give them directions.

Good thing I checked. They not only had me on the wrong road, but in the wrong county. If I had actually been choking on something, I would still be lying there.

I tried to describe to the dispatcher where I actually lived. I gave the big fancy fire number, GX304YM38B. That did no good.

Finally, I just said that I lived on the old Johnson place.

"Oh, the old Johnson place!" the lady said. "You mean the white house just down from the Erickson farm?"

Now it was all clear. The dispatcher found my farm in her plat book. She corrected her computer. When I finally have my heart attack, the ambulance crew will be able to find me.

Perhaps these new addresses make sense to somebody somewhere. One can only hope they make sense to the emergency people. It is even possible that it will make things easier for them.

But I doubt it. It is more likely that some bureaucrat with more power than brains decided that everybody should live on a street and have a house number just like him, whether it made any sense or not.

I suppose we'll get used to the new addresses, just like we got used to having to dial the prefixes on local phone numbers when that "improvement" came in. But no matter how insignificant the change, I miss living on Rural Route 1.

New Four Wheel Drive

Having a four-wheel-drive vehicle for the first time in my life has done wonders for my self-esteem. In fact, it has probably made me intolerable.

For six years I drove a two-wheel-drive pickup, one which I had to load down with firewood, sandbags or cement blocks in order to have a grip on icy roads. Now I just flip the switch into four wheel and step on it.

That is, until some moron with a two-wheel-drive gets in front of me at an intersection and sits there spinning. They should have a special lane for those people. Or just arrest them.

What a change. A couple of years ago, I was going to write a column about how they should force those jerks with front-wheel-drives and four-wheel-drives to drive only as fast as it is safe for the rest of us to drive.

For crying out loud, I thought at the time, you are driving on ice at a moderate speed with your shoulders tense as a snare drum, gripping the wheel with white knuckles—when some idiot with front wheel drive races by and whips up a cloud of snow that sends you into a complete whiteout.

Not fair, I thought. Those people should be arrested and forced to go through sensitivity training so they will be tolerant of the diversity of vehicles on the road, and realize that there are real human beings behind the wheels of those two wheel drive cars and pickups, people whose feelings might be hurt if they wrap their car around a light pole because they were blinded by a white cloud.

Well, now I have a four-wheel-drive. I bought the pickup because it had air conditioning and a nice stereo, but I find the four-wheel-drive part very useful in the winter. After years of relying on others to pull me out of the ditch, I can't wait to rescue somebody less fortunate than I with my new rig.

Yes, our ideals change as our situation changes. When I was in college I thought, boy, they better not raise tuition, that's not fair. All those rich business people should be glad to support us poor college students with their tax dollars.

Now that I am in business, my tune has changed. What those college students need when they start whining is a good swift kick. Maybe that'll teach them the value of a dollar.

My grandpa was against all government aid to anybody—until he got in the nursing home and ran out of money to pay for it. Suddenly, he was happy there was some socialism going on at the county and state level.

A person can't take one's ideas too seriously. They might change. Knowing that, I try to control my road rage. Who knows, I might again someday be stuck behind the wheel of a two-wheel-drive pickup at an icy intersection.

Daylight Savings Time

It is only an hour difference, but I get jet lag when we change to Daylight Savings Time. Suddenly, it is still dusk at ten past eight in the evening.

It took me several years to learn how to change the digital clock in my pickup. For the longest time, I just added the extra hour in my head during the summer. That worked pretty well, and saved the trouble of switching the clock back in the fall.

About a year ago, I found the directions for the clock underneath the front seat on the passenger side—right there with the gum wrappers, Kleenexes, dried up apples, half eaten candy bars and partially disintegrated survival candles.

Turns out you have to hold your thumb on the FM button for five seconds until the hour blinks, and then you hit "tune" to move the hour up or down. Then hold the FM button again for five seconds until the minutes blink, and do the same thing over.

Now, how are you supposed to figure that out? I now keep the directions in the glove compartment for reference every six months. But what a pain.

Supposedly, our former Gov. Orville Freeman lost his last election for governor because he came out in favor of Daylight Saving Time, which was regarded by some traditionalists as a communist-inspired threat to the American way of life.

The traditionalists were probably right. The time change has bitten me more than once, and I am starting to think it is a bad idea.

One recent October, I stayed out late on a Saturday night and thus permitted myself to sleep a little late Sunday morning. When I awoke, I remembered that there was a meatball dinner at one of the local churches starting at noon. It was just about noon.

I popped out of bed, showered, threw on some clothes, and rushed to the church. I burst through the door, hoping to load up my plate before they ran out of food.

But when I got in the door, there was no bustle of voices in the basement, no clanking of dishes. I had forgotten the time change! They were just starting the service. I was an hour early.

To make matters more complex, it was missionary Sunday and the guest missionary wasn't about to let earthly things like a meatball dinner keep him from going through all six hundred of his slides.

For over an hour I slumped in the back pew, weak from hunger, tired, bedraggled, heavy laden. Finally, I heard a loud whisper, "Psst, Eric!"

It was Alice, who was downstairs watching the meatballs. She had crept up the stairwell to see what the delay was, and decided to pull me out of the service.

"Sometimes they don't know when to quit," she said in disgust as we creaked down the stairs.

Alice dished me up. I have never tasted creamier mashed potatoes or more scrumptious Swedish meatballs. Absolutely heavenly. As Grandma used to say, all's well that ends well.

Never Alone

They keep coming out with more and more gadgets designed to keep us in eternal touch with everything and everybody. Answering machines. Pagers. Cell phones. E-mail. Hand-held computers.

Every new communications development complicates life a little more. I was trying on some jeans at the mall the other day and overheard a cell phone ring in the next cubicle. A man answered and said, "Sorry, you must have the wrong number."

Pestered by a wrong number in the changing room! That's a new one.

Now there is caller ID. That means those you call see your name on a screen before they answer. They are free not to pick up the phone if they don't like you. No answer could mean much more than it used to.

I think all of these communication devices make people lonelier than they were before.

Let me explain. It is one thing to be sitting in a log cabin in a national park reading a book knowing full well that nobody can reach you even if they try. That is solitude and it should be a joy.

It is another thing to have your laptop computer with you in the cabin, as well as your cell phone and your pager. With these gadgets present, you are connected. You are not truly alone, and it isn't good.

With communications devices in the room, if nobody calls,

sends you an e-mail, or pages you, instead of enjoying your time alone in the cabin, you begin to wonder, why is nobody calling me?

When surrounded by gadgets, instead of enjoying the solitude of being alone, you can feel as if you are in a room full of people and none of them are talking to you. Solitude is changed to loneliness.

Most people detest solitude. But I find that people who relish time alone are usually more interesting than those who have to be with people all of the time. Solitude can enrich the soul if one can learn to enjoy it. Electronic communication makes solitude rare.

Communication by gadget is no substitute for meeting face to face. Conversations mean more in person than they do over electronic devices. Frowns, twinkles in the eye, smiles, grimaces and gestures add meaning and flavor to what people say.

Letters last, as do memories of face-to-face conversations. Electronic communications disappear.

Electronic devices have the effect of tying us down to other humans without being able to enjoy their company. Such devices can also interrupt the natural and necessary breaks we get from each other when we are not in the same room.

Although many of these gadgets seem irresistible due to their alleged convenience, we might consider what they take away from us before we wire ourselves up from head to toe.

Online on the Farm

Much of this Internet hoopla is pure balderdash. People won't quit going to grocery stores. They aren't about to buy bread online. The malls will still be crowded between Thanksgiving and Christmas.

But, although I always try to be a skeptic, evidence is piling up that our lives will be changed forever by this technology, whether for better or for worse.

Recently a friend asked if I could find the lyrics and music to his favorite Bon Jovi song. I jumped on the Internet and in three minutes my printer was spewing out chord charts and lyrics to *Livin' on a Prayer,* all for free.

When I order widgets for the business from a supplier, I can check the supplier's widget inventory on the internet, which saves a call. And, I can order the widgets by e-mail, which saves another call.

On top of saving time, the Internet eliminates the needless chit-chat one usually must endure from widget company employees. That is surely a good thing.

You might be surprised how many people in the countryside trade stocks over the Internet. Many, especially women, are doing well, according to an investment magazine. Seems that women are finally able to act on their intuitions free of interference from the condescending but often incompetent males who control brokerage firms.

The Internet has become the world's largest auction, one

you can attend in your pajamas. From baseball cards to Van Gogh original paintings, you can find it for sale on the web and place your bid at 3 a.m. from the comfort of your own home.

If you need an obscure tractor part, say for a 1949 Allis Chalmers, you probably can find it on the Internet in a half-hour, or at least find the phone number of somebody who can help you.

I have found old college roommates, high school buddies, Bible camp friends from elementary school, all manner of people from my distant past, on the Internet. Usually we exchange brief life stories by e-mail and never write again. But a couple of dormant friendships have been rekindled, and others have been enriched by more frequent communication.

This Internet thing isn't going to go away. And it isn't only for tech-savvy city types. In fact, one of the joys of the Internet is that I can sit in my country home and find books, music, friends, entertainment, bargains, airplane tickets, the whole works, without having to drive 70 miles to the nearest city, and without even picking up the phone.

On the Internet, at least, one isn't punished for staying on the farm.

What's in a Name?

Hospitals used to be called sensible names like Fairview, Riverside, or the Fargo Hospital. Others were named after some saint. Banks were called First National, First State or First Federal.

Now we have non-word names for companies such as Alerus, Altru and Meritcare. Bell Atlantic just became Verizon. There is Quancor. Quipco. Citpac. Fizzwop. You can't even tell from these names what the company does.

These consultant-generated names are meant to convey false impressions, not information. We're supposed to get a good feeling from the nifty-sounding name, as if this huge corporation cares about us. Only later will we find out what they are going to do to our body, spirit, or pocketbook.

I think the corporate fuzz heads who came up with these uninformative names should be lined up against a brick wall and pelted with tomatoes. Hard, green tomatoes.

It is difficult to figure out where to visit somebody who is in the hospital. Herman Johnson's in intensive care at Alluva. But where is Alluva? Well, it used to be Altera. Where's that? Well, you know, they took over the old St. John's.

Oh! Now it makes sense. Except for that Alluva owns every hospital in the region, so they are all called Alluva. When you look in the phone book to call Alluva to ask about Herman, you have to figure out, which Alluva?

You call one place at a time until you discover Herman

was at the old St. Mary's. By then, he's been transferred to Sunnyview Nursing Home, or what is now called QualityCare Extended Living Facility.

That's not the worst of it. After these companies spend $500,000 for a consultant to come up with a name which means absolutely nothing but which market researchers claim will make people feel like they are smelling fresh bread, they spend another two million to put that horrible name on some sports stadium.

No more Candlestick Park. No more Ebbets Field, Polo Grounds or Three Rivers Stadium. Now we have 3Com Park, the Target Center, and Costco Field. Soon Yankee Stadium will become Pizza Hut Park.

Nobody objects to this brazen commercialization of darn near everything. People should come up with folk names for these stadiums, like "the barn," or "the big donut," and let the money go to waste. Instead, parents announce to their children that they are headed to Kmart Field, and the kids squeal with delight.

Maybe we could pump up our area economy a little by selling the naming rights to local institutions. I mean, wouldn't a Monsanto Lutheran Church with a new addition be better than a First Lutheran Church without? Wouldn't a Miller High Life Senior High with a swimming pool be better than Public School District #692 without?

Crusaders

Once upon a time, only people who lived in communes and ate granola recycled their garbage. Now, every Tom, Dick and Knute is separating glass from plastic and saving aluminum cans.

In fact, recycling has taken on religious significance. Many people seem to gain a sense of righteousness when they save a can, as if by doing so they have rescued a rare parakeet from extinction.

If you are callous enough to throw a can in the regular garbage, you are liable to get scolded in a Sunday School tone of voice: "We should really recycle those cans, now, shouldn't we?"

I once threw away an empty pop can in my own home, only to be scolded by house guests, who, up to that moment, were cherished friends. I told them they could take the can home with them. They did, cradling it as if it were an abandoned kitten.

People grab hold of any idea which gives them a feeling that they are, in whatever small way, better than other people. In the hands of people eager for a sense of superiority, recycling, which is undoubtedly a good idea, has degenerated into a moral crusade.

Smoking isn't a good idea, but I am uncomfortable with people who go on puritanical crusades to eradicate tobacco altogether. Why can't they be satisfied not to smoke themselves, and not to be exposed to smoke in public places?

No, anti-tobacco reformers dream of the day when they can even prevent people from sneaking out behind the barn for an occasional puff. That's going too far, and I am sure it is unpatriotic and unconstitutional.

I change my tune when it comes to seat belts. I don't wear mine unless threatened with a fine. Before North Dakota required that you wear seat belts, I couldn't get myself to buckle up until I was crossing the bridge into Minnesota, where seat belts were required.

I know several people who walk this earth who would not be alive if they hadn't been wearing their seat belts. So, I don't mind the state telling me to buckle up.

I also get peeved at these people who talk on their car phones while driving. I have nearly been run over by several of them. They were so busy chatting they never knew they had a close call.

If the state decides to arrest those morons, I won't mind a bit.

But, I don't want bureaucrats telling me where to put my empty Coke can.

CHAPTER SIX

MAIN STREET

Breakfast at the Cafe

A sure way to have a good day is to start out with a pancake and coffee at the local cafe. Every little town up here seems to have a place where the farmers and others gather before they head out for work.

Breakfast cafes which open at six in the morning are a Midwest tradition. When I have visited other parts of the country, I have found that standards for breakfast cafes are much lower.

Cafes in other parts of the country don't open as early. Their pancakes tend to be as dry and stiff as cardboard. No amount of butter and syrup can rescue a pancake with a hard outer crust.

The suburbs of the Twin Cities are no better. While visiting the cities a couple of years ago, I tried to find a local cafe for an early pancake. I started out at 7 a.m. Fifty-six miles and an hour-and-a-half later, I finally found a cafe in the decayed downtown of farm town surrounded by newly-developed sub-divisions.

If you leave the country completely, your chances at finding a pancake at six-thirty in the morning are virtually nil. I tried in New Zealand, England, and Poland. I usually ended up wandering around like a thirsty cow in the desert.

And so, early breakfast at a local cafe is one of the unique joys of rural Minnesota.

Breakfast cafes are a male domain. If a man is unlucky

enough to be accompanied by his wife to breakfast, the two will split up upon entering the cafe, like Quakers at church.

The woman goes off to the corner and joins a table of widows. Her husband is expected to ignore her completely until it is time to go, at which time he shuffles over to the widow's table and grunts a couple of times without making eye contact with his wife or any of the women at the table.

In their booths, the men discuss machinery, the blasted government, their car, or crops. The language is salty and tough. Looking at a menu is forbidden. Saying please or thank you to the waitress is not permitted. Tipping is frowned upon.

In fact, the waitress should really know what you want ahead of time. If you are anybody at all, the cook will pour your cake on the grill thirty seconds after you enter the door.

It is okay to help yourself to the coffee pot, but if you do, you are obligated to make the rounds and fill everybody's cup before putting the pot back on the warmer. The overworked waitress is then expected to apologize for not doing her job.

Breakfast carries on until one person gets up and says, "Well, I suppose." A couple of others say, "Yup, it's about that time," which means breakfast is adjourned and it's time to get to work.

Unless you are retired, in which case breakfast merges into morning coffee, which can fade into the noon meal, which can turn into afternoon coffee, and so on.

County Fair

Going to the county fair would be less difficult if I could just figure out how to deal with the clumsy social situations which come up every few steps.

It is fun to see all of the familiar people, but how do you know whether to stop and talk, or whether it is enough to smile, wave, and keep on walking? If you stop to talk, how do you know when it is safe to excuse yourself and walk away?

At the last county fair I attended, I set out across the midway. I immediately ran into my neighbors Herb and Arlene. We see each other often enough, but they were curious whether my current blinked off the other night like theirs did. We're on the same line, so we often talk about current affairs, pardon the pun.

While discussing blinking alarm clocks with Herb and Arlene, along comes a classmate from high school. I turned to talk to the classmate, whom I hadn't seen in nineteen years, leaving Herb and Arlene in the lurch.

Now, should I have introduced Herb and Arlene to the classmate? I didn't. They eventually drifted away, probably quite offended by my rudeness.

I was now stuck visiting with my classmate. I soon found out he was no more interesting now than he had been when we barely knew each other in high school.

The classmate was carrying on about his consulting business when up walked Mrs. Bjornson, my old Sunday school teacher. A big hug, and a new social dilemma. What do I do about this classmate, who is now standing there kicking the dust? I tried to wriggle my way out of the situation with body language. I put my arm around Mrs. Bjornson just to let her know she wasn't being ignored, and I asked the classmate some lame questions about his very important-sounding consulting firm.

In the middle of his first sentence, I spotted a college buddy out of the corner of my eye. I waved, and he came right over for some back-slapping, how ya doin, all that buddy stuff–and yet more stress.

Now I was juggling my consultant classmate, my Sunday school teacher, who had just been prattling on about how I had been such a good little boy, and my college friend who, if he opened his big mouth, would make it obvious that I have not always been such a good little boy.

The high school classmate finally gave up on his story, waved sadly and walked away with his head down much like he had back in third grade when nobody would teeter totter with him because he was fat.

Mrs. Bjornson, sensing sin in the air, excused herself.

Having offended four people in five minutes, I turned to my college buddy only to find that he had already found somebody more interesting to talk to. Now I was the one left kicking the dirt.

All of this made me wish for a recliner, a good book, and three feet of snow.

Rumor Mill

One curious fact about small towns: Everybody hates the gossip, yet everybody with a pulse does it.

In fact, if a person claims never to gossip, I take it as a sign that they will lie about other things, too.

It is easy to be self-righteous about not spreading gossip, especially when one gets burned by the rumor mill. But when push comes to shove, who can pass up the chance to spread a little bit of juicy news? Almost nobody.

Gossip in small towns is inevitable if only because there are so many colorful characters there. Telling stories about the locals can be pure fun. I mean, if Jimbo gets drunk and climbs the water tower, what are we supposed to do—treat it like some secret?

But a darker force pushes on most gossip: People are desperate to make themselves look good, even at the expense of others. Deep down, most people fear that they don't fit in. Gossiping makes them feel like an insider.

As people get older, some give up gossiping completely. But others give themselves over to gossip as a full-time profession. Their workplace is the cafe. Their paycheck comes the first of the month.

I admire those who rise above gossip as they age. They are the wise ones. They often have suffered from being misunderstood themselves. When they hear gossip, they are more suspicious of the rumor's source than they are of the rumor's victim.

But at the same time, I don't want to be too hard on those of us who gossip. Gossipers are usually driven by inner demons. They are more to be pitied than reviled. They often have nothing else to do.

Want to feel small? Try winning the approval of somebody in a position of high responsibility, somebody you admire, by reporting some gossip. If they've been around the block, they'll ignore you. I've tried this. Gossip always falls flat with accomplished people.

Turns out, truly important people get to be important by rising above pettiness. They become admired by getting to the bottom of things, by sifting out the trivial from what matters, and by insisting upon the truth.

Not only do admirable people avoid spreading gossip, but they seem to have no fear of the rumor mill. They listen to the beat of their own drum. They realize that to fear gossip is to give gossipers too much credit. They know that gossip about themselves is usually harmless and that gossipers are probably just jealous.

It seems that people who really go places realize that being a victim of gossip is almost always a position of high honor. After all: If you aren't up, nobody will bother tearing you down.

Tire Squealers

One recent evening I was jolted out of my sleep by the squeal of a car laying a strip of rubber down on the highway.

Now, I don't know who the driver was. I didn't bother to get up to see if I recognized the car. But I think we can rule out several segments of the population as possible perpetrators.

First, you can eliminate females. I have never known a female to squeal tires late at night just for the sheer joy of squealing tires. As much as I would love to see a perfectly coifed gray-haired Lutheran lady squeal through town in a souped up GTO with the stereo going boom, boom, boom, that was not likely the case here.

We can also eliminate males under sixteen and over twenty-five. Those under sixteen aren't supposed to be driving. We hope. As for those over twenty-five, the insurance companies know that something happens at twenty-five which makes males stop squealing their tires. They wouldn't lower the car insurance rates for men so drastically at age 25 otherwise.

We are left with males ages 16-24 as the possible tire squealers.

What a bunch. Ever eager to prove themselves but without the sense to realize the consequences of their actions, this age group of males does more damage to roads, cars, and public property than the rest of the population combined.

They even wreck their own property in efforts to prove their toughness. I mean, what is damaged by squealing tires other than the tires and transmission of the owner's car? That obvious truth, as well as many others, is slow to sink in with this group.

During those years, males know it all, even if they know nothing. They brim with confidence, nearly all of it unjustified.

They fill our prisons. If there's havoc, they've wreaked it. If there are skid marks on the highway, wheel tracks on the lawn, mailboxes bashed, gravestones tipped, or spray paint on the water tower, you can bet it was a male between the ages of 16 and 24 who was the ringleader.

So, what should we do about this? Lock all males up for six years when they turn eighteen?

That won't work. We need young males around to lift heavy things, fight wars, and play on the sports teams for our entertainment. And not all of them are bad apples.

There is probably no answer better than what the older people say when they hear squealing tires or the rap of loud engine pipes: "Kids," they say, with a shake of their head. "Young and dumb."

Perhaps many older people quietly envy the naive, carefree confidence of youth, even at its most stupid and destructive. They remember with fondness such spontaneity in themselves, and they know it will soon be crushed.

Remodeling

I have spent the past winter on a remodeling project at my little business. I can safely say that I would prefer a root canal.

A root canal is over in one day and it comes with codeine. Remodeling is a chronic illness.

One thing leads to another. We needed rest rooms, but that meant moving the office, which meant moving the lunch area, which meant moving the check-out counter.

Bathrooms, you say? That led some snoop to ask about the septic system. Turns out the tank was put in before the last world war and was probably leaking raw sewage into the neighbor's well.

I had imagined that the carpenters would show up, throw up a few walls and then boom, everything would be finished. Suddenly, we had backhoes ripping up the entire yard to install the mother of all septic systems.

A little later I found myself in the middle of a heated debate over which grade of gravel to use for fill under the slab. The gravel man said he had a pile of cheap stuff ready to go at the Johnson pit, but it was Class 17. That might do, said the cement man, but he'd rather have Class 9. The carpenter figured Class 5 would pack better. The plumber wanted fine sand.

After saying their piece, they all took a pull on their cigarettes and looked to me for a ruling. Knowing nothing about gravel, upper or lower class, I bluffed.

"Let's do it right!" I said with authority. "I want nothing but first class! Haul in first class gravel and be done with it!"

That caused them to agree on one thing: I didn't know squat.

Carpenters, electricians and plumbers all share a fondness for one phrase: "By the time you pay me to fiddle around with this old stuff, you might just as well have put in all new."

Early on, I said yes, put in all new. Yep, go ahead, get it over with. Tear out that old thing and put in a new thing. Might as well do it right. No use to skimp.

Then the bills poured in for the new things. What a jolt! If this is saving money, I said to myself, what is spending money like?

I ran to the banker with the stack of bills. "We've started a monster, and we don't know how to stop it!" I said, expecting some concern.

The banker just laughed. He'd seen it all before. Loaning me enough money to put me in hock until I collect Social Security didn't seem to bother him at all.

I walked out of the bank in pain, wishing I had saved a couple of those codeine pills from the last root canal.

In Pursuit of Drain Tile

Ah, the fun of doing business in a small town. My recent search for a 35-foot stretch of perforated four-inch plastic drain tile took me further than I had ever dreamed.

The carpenters informed me that they needed this tile and fast. I called the local sewer man to see if he had any on hand.

No, said the sewer man. The lumber yard has drain tile, but they won't sell you any less than a 100-foot roll. Kind of a waste. He thought for a bit. You know, he said, Swenson south of town had some extra from his septic project last year, maybe you should give him a call.

Swenson had only 15 feet, so I called the sewer man back. "Meet me at the shop in the morning," he said.

I had no idea what this drain tile was going to cost. Every time I asked about price, the sewer man said he had no idea. It sounded bad.

The next day, I dragged myself to the sewer man's shop before sunrise. Pickup after pickup pulled up to the shop. The coffee was on. Somebody brought donuts.

The sewer man sipped his coffee, deep in thought. Finally, in a break between hunting stories, he turned towards the man who brought the donuts. "Hey, Gordo, you have some drain tile left from last spring, don't you?"

Sure enough, Gordon had a 50-foot stretch of black four-inch perforated drain tile in his barn. I vaguely knew of Gordo, mainly because his bachelor party 20 years ago is a local legend. He jumped into his Silverado and I followed him 10 miles out to his farm.

We dragged the tile from the back of the barn. Cats scurried in all directions. I stuffed the tile in my pickup while Gordon disappeared into the house to figure out the price. I was prepared for the worst.

Minutes passed. No Gordo. I watched the sunrise. I watched the cats fight over their food. I got to know the dog. Finally, Gordo poked his head out the door and told me to come in.

The floor of the entry was covered in crumpled receipts from the lumber yard. Hundreds of slips. Gordo was trying to find the one for the tile. No luck.

Finally, he had an idea. "I'll disguise my voice and call the lumber yard."

Turns out, a 100-foot roll of drain tile would cost $34. For Gordon's fifty-foot stretch, we figured $17 would be fair. I counted out the cash, and the transaction was complete.

All of this rigamarole to save $17, you might say. But in the pursuit of a little drain tile, I got a donut and a cup of coffee. I heard some good hunting stories. I saw the inside of Gordo's barn. And best of all, I get to brag that I got a good deal.

Mowing

People in rural Minnesota sure love to mow their lawns. The mowing impulse has a lot to do with the prevalence of northern Europeans in this area. Swedes, Norwegians and Germans are notoriously neat.

Going west, the quality of lawns declines quickly after one crosses the Missouri River. By the time you get to ranch country, people just don't care. "Live and let live," is their motto, and it applies equally to grass and people.

Towns with a half-dozen Lutheran churches are always neatly mowed. Catholics have nice lawns, too, with a greater emphasis on statuary and a little less oppressive orderliness.

But go to areas where Lutherans and Catholics are replaced by Baptists, Pentecostals and other sects, the grass can get pretty sloppy.

You can tell a lot about people by their lawns. When I see a yard with a tightly clipped lawn and shrubs clipped into little round balls, my first thought is, what would it like to be these people's child?

Something tells me that for every oppressively neat yard out here in the country, there are grown children in the suburbs with large therapy budgets.

On the opposite end of the spectrum, when people slide into moral laxity, their lawn is usually the first to go. "They just let the grass grow," the neighbors say, which is a nice way of hinting that Herbert has started drinking again, or that the

Albertsons are fighting once more, or that drugs are being dealt on the premises.

People who are retired but still healthy, or who are trapped in cubicles all day slaving away for a faceless company, or who have to deal with the public, or who are sick and tired of listening to their kids, often turn to mowing for solace.

When relatives come for an extended visit, you can't very well announce that you are going to leave the house because you just need to spend some time alone. But it is perfectly acceptable etiquette to say, "I have to go mow."

I often wonder what the story is behind some of these huge lawns. For instance, what would cause somebody who lives along a country highway to keep expanding their lawn into the ditch?

Some aren't satisfied with a little bit of the road ditch. They expand their lawns deep into the ditch, far along the road, even beyond their own property. I have measured one local lawn-ditch that runs for nine-tenths of a mile. You wonder, is there a frustrated Julius Caesar at work here, driven to conquer and tame new territory?

I suspect that people's motives for mowing are usually pretty simple. In a busy world where things don't often go right, where jobs can be a drag, and where people are unreliable, mowing the lawn is a good way to feel as if you have accomplished something.

Local Clinic

One disadvantage of having a local clinic is that you know everybody in the waiting room. Often a neighbor who is slightly hard of hearing figures he just has to know what is wrong with you. You try to mumble and gesture, but when they yell, "Speak up!" you have to spill the beans at full volume.

At that point, I usually announce that I am suffering from an enlarged phlebula. I don't know what a phlebula is, but nobody else does either. It usually puts a stop to the interrogation.

Doctor visits have terrified me since childhood. My gag reflex is over-sensitive, so the thing I fear the most at the doctor's office is the wooden tongue depressor. When the doctor reaches into the jar to pull one out before looking down my throat, I panic.

"I won't need one of those," I say in a quivering voice, "I'll open real wide."

I then pretend I am a python trying to swallow a muskrat. The doctor compliments me every time. "Goodness, what a big mouth we have today!"

Unlike most people, I don't mind spending time in the waiting room, as long as the magazines are interesting. Usually there are periodicals like *People* or *McCall's*, to which I would never subscribe, but which are worth paging through once every six months or so.

Some waiting rooms never get new magazines. They

should. When I get stuck with a 1987 copy of *Retirement Illustrated*, I get antsy and start nagging the receptionist to get me in before I fall over dead.

Nagging the receptionist does no good. To get rid of me, she just puts me in the examining room for 45 minutes. The magazines in there are even older. The *Physician's Desk Reference* seems off limits. The full color wall posters of the intestinal tract make me feel even sicker.

Sitting there all alone, I get creative ideas. For example, I get a kick out of cleaning my ears with those 8-inch wooden Q-tips.

A few years back, after paging through the old *Guidepost* and the *Country Living,* I mustered the courage to pull a stunt I had always wanted to try: I grabbed onto those two stainless steel loops at the end of the examining table and attempted a headstand.

Suddenly, I heard the doctor grab the chart outside the door. He whooshed into the room to find me in an odd position for a sick person. I sheepishly explained that the blood to my head relieved my symptoms.

Unfazed, the doctor ordered me to repeat the procedure four times per day on an empty stomach.

CHAPTER SEVEN

FOUR SEASONS

Warm Spell

Our little February spring ended with an early March jolt, but people don't seem to mind. After record warm temperatures, we are now back to normal. It is kind of a relief.

In fact, hitting sixty degrees in late February felt almost immoral. As you tip-toe around outside waiting for the other shoe to drop, you begin to wonder what will be the consequences of the unseasonably warm weather. When will we be punished?

During the warm spell, I overheard more than a few people predicting a hot, dry summer, perhaps the beginning of a long drought. Sixty degrees in early March? Boy, that must mean we'll get 102 degrees in July.

If you look deeply enough, you can find a dark lining to any silver cloud. People around here are experts at finding that dark lining, even on a sixty degree day in February.

"It's sure been nice," people say, sounding almost afraid. To make sure they don't sound too excited, some quickly add, with a sad shake of the head:

"Yep, it's probably gonna kill the alfalfa."

Or, the warm weather will get the tulips. Or the strawberries. Or the lilacs. Or the snowmobile factory. Or the ski resorts. There is always a downside, and people feel duty bound to point it out.

There is a law etched in the minds and spirits of Minnesotans: Pleasure now means pain later. Good weather now means drought this summer, or too much rain, or a killing

June frost. Whatever. Something bad is going to happen if this good weather holds out.

I remember the first time I escaped Minnesota's winter. I was twenty-eight years old. I rode Amtrak to Arizona.

When I stepped off the train into that sunshine and warmth, I felt like a new person. I had seen Arizona's temperature readings on the weather map, but until I felt the sun on my face, I didn't really believe there was a place on earth that felt that warm in January.

It took me days to get over the guilt of escaping the frozen north. Wasn't there something wrong with cheating winter? What would happen to me to compensate?

Despite my worries, the other shoe never dropped. I stayed for weeks. Nothing bad happened. I enjoyed myself more with each passing day.

I learned a tough lesson: People who live in warm climates aren't punished for missing winter like you would think they should be. The spoiled brats reap the rewards of their climate without penalty.

When warm weather arrived last week, I resolved to ignore my doom and gloom impulses and enjoy the warmth while it lasted. I even went so far as to barbecue some burgers on the deck.

Of course a blizzard hit the next day, wouldn't you know.

The Melt

We seem stuck in early spring, the most excruciating time of year. If the weather is warm, you have mud. If it is cold, it feels like spring will never come. In between are ice and slush. Hopes of thaw are repeatedly raised and then dashed.

Snow banks start to melt, but only enough to reveal five month's worth of beer cans, candy wrappers, dead cats, lost gloves, and grease and grime. When it gets cold again, the whole sordid mess freezes in place for another week.

The extended forecast predicts fifty degrees five days from now, but the weather gremlins continually postpone the warm-up. The promise of warmth hangs out there like a carrot on a stick.

The zipper on my winter coat went kaflooie a month ago. I resolved then not to get it fixed until next winter. But the cold continues, so I have been dressing in layers of lighter coats.

The firewood pile in the basement is nearly gone, and I won't replenish it. The furnace can take over until it gets warm out. The first fire of late fall is sure a lot more cozy than the last fire of early spring.

It's useless to wash the pickup because it'll just get covered with mud again the next warm day. And why clean up the entry? It will be a mess of little black puddles ten minutes after the next person trudges in.

All right, let's quit complaining and look at the good side:

The candy wrappers will soon disintegrate, the beer cans will be gathered up by the good citizens listed on the blue adopt-a-highway signs, and the dead cats will become crow food.

The last ice on the north side of the garage will disappear, the tulips on the south side of the house will push through, the Twins will start the season in a first place tie, and the chickadees will be replaced by robins and mourning doves.

The big tractors will soon roar over the fields. You sort of wonder who can still afford to put in crops, but spring is a season of eternal hope.

Finally, the lawns will green up. The drone of the first lawnmower will produce the first whiff of fresh cut grass, which truly wakes one up from winter.

The sun now sets directly at the end of the east-west roads, the clock has sprung ahead, and most basketball leagues have crowned their champion.

Coming up soon is that window of time where one can wander around outside past sunset without freezing or getting attacked by mosquitoes.

Spring Bustle

After winter's stillness, suddenly we have the bustle of spring. Birds start chirping at four something in the morning. The leaves grow larger each day. The dandelions bloom faster than the rabbits can eat them.

The flowering crabs have started to open. The lilacs come next. I saw a spirea in full bloom yesterday, May 6th. The asparagus should be up, although I haven't had time to go out to check. The plum blossoms are completely open. Their scent is intoxicating.

At nine o'clock at night this time of year, it is still daylight. The birds still chirp. The farmers keep going around in their fields. People sit on their porch and visit.

Spring is just plain too much at once! At the same time everything else is growing and changing, we humans have to work hard as well, so hard that many of us don't get a chance to really watch things grow.

Nothing happens in January, nothing changes. When we have ample time to contemplate the meaning of existence, there is little or nothing to watch. If there were some lilacs blooming or some birds chirping, winter might not be so depressing.

I wonder how we can avoid missing spring because we are too busy doing spring work. One could move to New Zealand for the winter. Their summer runs through December, January and February. If one worked it right, you could have three springs in a year. They don't let foreigners work in New Zealand, so one would have plenty of time to sit around and watch things bloom.

But flights to kiwi country are long and expensive. And their plants are unfamiliar.

Early retirement for the purpose of enjoying spring isn't an option. Nothing is more sad than to watch retired farmers creep around the countryside in their Park Avenues watching other farmers seed. They don't want to sniff the lilacs. They long to smell the diesel fumes again!

Stop to think of it, I did have one spring where I was unable to work. I went to Poland to study history one May. We spent an hour per day in the classroom, and the rest of the time we were free to walk around Warsaw's many parks. We had no homework.

Turns out, watching nature got boring after about three days. Yes, it was nice to amble around and enjoy the Polish spring, which is much like ours, but something was missing.

It didn't feel right to have spring without being dead tired at the end of a long day of work. I got lazy. I started sleeping in until class started. I gained ten pounds.

The birds sang and the lilacs bloomed. The leaves grew each day, and the grass was fresh. But without any work to do, spring started to feel a lot like winter!

March Madness

In Minnesota, March usually comes in like a lion and goes out like a leopard. The only thing lamb-like about our March weather is the snow that is white as fleece.

March can dish out a couple of healthy storms and sometimes a blizzard. Tantalizing thaws are followed by bone-chilling cold. Frozen slush makes it dangerous to walk.

And diseases. It seems that when the temperature outside hovers around freezing, the little microbes that cause coughs, ear aches and sore throats are more active. That is my theory. I can be healthy all winter, but when it starts to thaw, look out. March's misery is made more bearable because we know that the melt is around the corner. The Twins are in spring training. Basketball is well into the tournaments. The sun stays up way past supper. And Lent is in full swing.

Boy, once the snow melts, I tell myself, I am going to milk this summer for all it is worth. I am going to spend most of my time outside. I am going to raise enough vegetables to fill a deep freeze. I am going to travel to Montana to hike in the mountains.

I am going to clear a trail through the woods. I am going to run a couple of miles per day. I am going to go canoeing on some of these nice lakes around here that I never use. I am going to get out my ball and glove and get the old arm back in shape.

Yep, I am going to finally learn how to pound a nail and

then I'll build a deck. I am going to get up early every morning to see the sunrise, maybe go to town for a pancake before work. I am going to barbecue outside every other night.

I am going to go to several Twins games, hit Rollag on Labor Day, go to the Renaissance festival, take in the Winnipeg Folk Festival, and see the Boundary Waters for the first time. Oh, I've never been to Medora. I probably should do that on the way to Montana.

I won't miss a single county fair, street fair, food fair or the state fair. And how can I say I've lived if I've never been to We Fest? This is the year! Chill the beer!

I am afraid these ambitious plans neglect some crucial factors. First, mosquitoes. I forgot about them. So, you can cancel the garden, the running, the trail in the woods, and the canoeing.

Second, hay fever. That does away with We Fest and Rollag.

Third, humidity. Cross off the barbecues. Forget getting up at sunrise, that's the only time it is cool enough to sleep decently.

Oh, and work! I suppose one has to do that, too. Summer work makes one too tired to even think about the Boundary Waters.

In fact, on most summer evenings its nicest just to sit back and read a book. Just like in the winter.

Frost Boils

Most of the so-called big questions in life can't be researched, will never be answered, or are matters of speculation and are therefore best ignored. People who take life's big questions too seriously cause wars.

But there are a few little things I really would like to find out, and perhaps modern science can provide the answer.

For example, what causes gravel roads to form washboards? It is eerie how orderly those ridges on ungraded gravel roads can become with nothing else forming them but the wheels of countless cars. Give somebody a grant so we can figure this out!

Why does frost boil? Last week, a frost boil in our driveway pushed up a pile of mud almost two feet high. The inside of our pole shed is a muddy swamp, despite being on high ground. Frost boils are the culprit, I am told by people older and wiser.

There is one spot on the highway to town that gets rough every spring. Frost boils. Why can't they just dig out the whole road, put in new dirt and tar it over again? Wouldn't that fix it, or would there still be frost boils?

If there isn't a Frost Boil Research Institute, there should be. It could be funded by taxpayers from Florida. Frost boil research would be of more value to us up here than a dozen military bases. Even if they don't figure out how to stop frost boils, maybe they can explain them.

Another mystery: How can entire flocks of blackbirds take

off all at the same time and swerve at the very same instant? Which one is their leader? Why do they turn when they do? Which one decides where they are going to land?

Social scientists should study the group decision making processes of blackbird flocks. Do they brainstorm? Do they break into small groups and share? Do they use parliamentary procedure? If they do, they do it quick.

How do the same pair of geese find my swamp again every spring after traveling thousands of miles? More importantly, how do the two of them put up with each other on those long trips? Do they ever argue about where they are going to stop for the night? Which one usually wins?

How do those worms know when their fifteen years in hiding are up and they can come out and eat all of the leaves on the trees again? How do they count the fifteen years? Do any of them rebel and come out in twelve years? What is the punishment?

How does a bunch of ants figure out where to make a hill? How do bees reach agreement on where to put a hive? Do pocket gophers come out and play at night, or are they always underground?

These are some of life's little questions. I find them far more fascinating than the big questions, perhaps because there is the slim possibility we might someday find the answer.

June and the Dome

Kaboom, it's mid June. After waiting forever for the snow-drifts to melt and the trees to leaf and the temperatures to warm, now it's all here, and it's moving too fast.

June just plain gives us too much to drink in. Everywhere you turn there is lush green grass, blooming flowers, and deep shade under the large-leafed trees. The days are so long that one can't make use of all the hours of sunshine. The birds begin to chirp at 4 a.m.

Isn't it sinful to sit inside on these beautiful June evenings? What we would give for one such evening in January!

One week ago I went against my principles and spent a beautiful June evening inside the biggest room in Minnesota, the Metrodome, watching our Twins play Cleveland.

Baseball inside is not baseball. Its more like pinball. Too much loud music. Stupid mascots. Huge scoreboards. The baseball bounces unnaturally off the plastic turf.

Even the longest home runs lose their grandeur when you must watch the baseball skim past the teflon roof on its way over the plexiglass and plastic wall.

For all of my love of the game of baseball, when I actually attend a game I seldom know the score or even watch the action. There is simply too much other stuff going on, even inside the dome.

I like to sit in centerfield with a pair of binoculars and focus on the managers in the dugout. Or I watch just one player, say the right fielder, to see how he reacts to each play. Is his head in the game? What is he chewing? Why did he move five steps to his left before the last pitch?

When baseball is played outdoors, there is even more to distract one from the game on the field. A plane might fly over. There could be a thunderstorm brewing over the left field fence. Flocks of pigeons might land on the light towers.

If you're lucky, a full moon will rise over the centerfield fence in time for the seventh inning stretch. The air gets heavy as the evening cools, and the green grass glows under the lights.

But in the Metrodome, there are no such natural diversions. Last week, I found that by the sixth inning, I was played out. The lights were too bright. My eyes were sore. The music was too loud. The pitchers weren't throwing strikes. And it was beautiful outside.

So, I left.

Wouldn't you know, one inning later, Cristian Guzman of the Twins produced what announcers later called "the most exciting play of the season," a bunt which got away from the Indians allowing the speedy Guzman to circle the bases.

So, for the most exciting play of the season, I was outside in the parking lot, enjoying the outdoors, trying to squeeze all I could out of the month of June.

Hot Spell

Everything has a purpose, or so I have heard. So, let us search for a purpose behind this recent wave of heat and humidity.

If the heating and cooling people were short of business before, they aren't now. I have put off installing air conditioning for the past three cool summers. I figured I would only use it five days per year.

No longer. Something has to happen here. This is ridiculous. It is nearly 11 p.m. and I am pouring with sweat. The prospects for sleep tonight are not good. Money is no object. What are credit cards for? I am calling tomorrow.

The air is wet and stagnant, heavy with the rich smell of weed pollen. My glasses fog up when I open the fridge. Condensation pours from the toilet tank. Central Air, How I Long to Feel Thy Breezes Blow!

It is clear that the sultry weather is good for the heating and cooling sector. But what good does this week-long sauna do for the rest of us?

The heat makes us forget how bad winter is, that's what it does. With my bare back stuck to the back of this vinyl chair and my glasses slid to the end of my nose for the fortieth time today, I can actually bear the thought of twenty below zero.

This afternoon I heard a well-respected and reputedly sane person utter out loud in public the following phrase: "Boy, I sure wouldn't mind seeing some snow."

Six months ago, those words would have ruined the gentleman's good standing in the community. Today, his sentiments were immediately seconded and approved by a unanimous voice vote of all three present.

About this time of year we start to think, what's so bad about winter anyway?

Cold weather can invigorate. Head outside for a little bit, shovel the walk, trudge up for the mail, brush off the car, pop back in the house, stomp off the snow, peel off the layers, heat up some hot chocolate, toss another log on the fire. Sounds like fun.

Light a candle, wrap up in a quilt, read a book, throw on an extra afghan, go to bed early. That's what winter's all about.

Remember how the snow pack crunches when you back your vehicle out of the garage? What a cozy, nostalgic, relaxing sound. Maybe next winter I will record it.

What fun to punch through a fresh drift with my four wheel drive. I can't wait to risk my life running to town for milk in a blizzard. Storm warnings, cancellations, sunsets before supper, lost gloves, Christmas shopping on icy streets, none of it sounds too bad.

The heat has a purpose. It takes the edge off the memory of winter's worst.

At the same time, the heat threatens to make us forget that the corn on the cob is ripe, the garden is full of tomatoes, the flowers are in full bloom, the Twins are in first place, the Vikings look tough, and harvest is underway.

Corn on the Cob

August is the season for corn on the cob. Few foods taste better than fresh sweet corn picked a little bit on the white side, dripping in butter. I like to eat up to ten cobs in a sitting.

My grandfather used to plant way more sweet corn than we needed. As it started to ripen, he enlisted me to help build a fortress of chicken netting around the corn patch to keep the raccoons out.

What a job. Grandpa enjoyed fighting off the raccoons but I didn't think much of the annual project. Chicken netting is stubborn to deal with, especially when you are in sixth grade and would rather be riding your bike.

The raccoons always got into the corn patch anyway. The morning after their raids, Grandpa would roust me out of bed to help him strengthen the barricade. We tacked the netting to the ground every few feet and wired shut any openings.

When our repairs didn't work, and they never did, Grandpa would add a transistor radio tuned to the hardest rock station on the AM dial. It blared all night. The Rolling Stones didn't deter the raccoons for long, either.

One year, after all else failed, we sprinkled cayenne pepper on each tassel to make the raccoons sneeze. The pepper worked and it made Grandma happy, too. The little tin of cayenne had been gathering dust on her spice rack since the Eisenhower administration. Finally, it was put to good use.

Grandpa ate corn on the cob like a pit bull would eat raw

sirloin. You knew not to interrupt him. When he dove in, kernels flew in all directions. The butter made many kernels stick to his face.

Grandpa was always inviting visitors in for meals. No matter how dignified the guest, be it a traveling evangelist, the state Farm Bureau president, or the Fuller Brush man, Grandpa ate his corn the same way. When he looked up from his plate, his face was covered in corn and nobody dared tell him to clean it off.

I am the same way. Corn on the cob happens so seldom, why not enjoy it when it is here? We can mind our manners in January.

But I refuse to grow the stuff. I do not care to fight with the raccoons. If Grandpa were here, he would think I was soft and destined to go broke. But why go through the hassle of peppering tassels when you can get fresh corn for a couple bucks a dozen at the roadside stand?

Raking Leaves

The quest to rake up that last leaf has begun. Most of the leaves have fallen, but the cottonwoods, willows and a few other trees are slow to drop, which must infuriate the neat types who can't stand to see a single leaf on their lawn.

I don't rake my leaves. If I lived in town, I am sure they would have a neighborhood meeting and try to get an ordinance passed forcing me to rake.

If you just leave the leaves, the ones which don't blow away disappear after the first couple of mowings in the spring. The ground up leaves form humus, which is good for the lawn.

At least that is how I justify letting the leaves lie.

Leaf piles were a great joy when I was a kid. Well, they are even fun now. As I go up for the mail, I walk through the deepest leaves I can find, sliding my feet along so the rustling leaves make as much noise as possible.

I used to rake leaves just for the fun of burning the pile. Once the fire got started, it was fun to throw a bunch more leaves on top to try to smother the flames. The pile would stop smoking for a while, but eventually a little smoke would curl up in the middle. Suddenly the whole pile would burst into a bigger inferno than before.

Of course you aren't supposed to burn leaves anymore. There goes that reason for raking.

One time I gathered a huge pile of leaves and took a flying leap into them from atop the picnic table. Bad idea. Leaves don't make much of a cushion. I landed with a big thud. I haven't tried that one since.

Most of the leaves on our farm are from oaks. Oak leaves are crisp, firm and noisy. Maple leaves are leathery, but make up for their lack of texture by being the most colorful of them all. Cottonwood leaves are rubbery and sticky and don't burn easily.

Raking the leaves, whether necessary or not, gives people a chance to accomplish something outdoors in the beautiful fall weather. It is a ritual which people are hesitant to give up, even when they get too frail to do it themselves.

Falling and fallen leaves are a big part of this nostalgic time of year. The harvests are in, the gardens are tilled for next spring, the firewood is piled high, and the World Series is in full swing.

So, even though I no longer rake my leaves, I enjoy their smell and their sound. I enjoy when somebody breaks the law and starts one of their piles on fire. It all makes me thirsty for hot chocolate.

Winter Predictions

Last week I heard a new theory on how to predict the severity of the upcoming winter: the acorn crop. Apparently, the more acorns, the more ugly a winter we will have. One wonders, what do the oak trees know that we don't?

This year several of our oaks have dropped loads of acorns, but in most places the acorn crop is pretty thin. Southern Minnesota, where I picked up this nutty tidbit of folk wisdom, has a huge acorn crop, so I guess they'll get clobbered good and proper.

Other possible early-warning winter indicators: The width of the stripe on caterpillars, the thickness of the walls of muskrat houses, the Farmer's Almanac, the earliness of the geese migration, and the number of winter coats sold at J. C. Penney.

Like Uncle Jake's arthritic knee, none of these indicators has ever been wrong, so they say.

Okay, let us turn back the clock to last year at this time. Everybody was predicting doom. Yep, supposed to be a bad one, worse than 1997. No matter to whom people attributed the prediction, they added the phrase, "...and they've never been wrong."

But I don't remember having much winter last winter. In fact, I recall going out to the lake for a suntan on February 8th. It was sixty-four degrees. There was one night in mid-December with low visibility on the roads. That's it. At most, there were ten days of real cold.

The doom sayers were wrong. Doom sayers in all areas of life are usually wrong, but they never seem to lose their credibility. There will always be a market for doom.

Does anybody call the false prophets on the carpet when their predictions are wrong? I try. I recall that there were scads of acorns on the ground last fall, just before the winter that wasn't winter. So, I did my duty and told the person with the acorn theory that he was nuts.

He ignored me and presented even more theories, like anybody with a theory would. Yep, the ocean currents have never been this screwed up. The ants have never had bigger hills. The jet stream is getting all messed up by those jets flying around up there.

Global warming is another popular theory. Unlike folk wisdom about acorns and the upcoming winter, global warming theories come with the endorsement of scientists and their computers.

Don't get me wrong, I am all for global warming. If it's happening, fine with me. But there probably isn't much to it. Average temperatures have fluctuated wildly over the centuries.

In fact, they found a fossil of a palm tree out in North Dakota a couple of weeks ago. There must have been some wicked global warming at some time for a palm to grow this far north. Let's hope it happens again!

Winter Driving

During the summer, I promise myself not to drive in bad weather next winter. When winter comes, however, our minds work differently. Inevitably I find myself out in dangerous conditions, usually for no good reason.

After working outside all day in the summer, one's house is a refuge in the evenings. It is a joy to sit back in the recliner and turn on a Twins game.

But after spending all day inside during the winter, one's house seems like a prison. You can't open the windows. It gets dark so early that six o'clock is indistinguishable from eleven o'clock. Watching television doesn't have the same appeal.

Even reading is no fun when one gets cabin fever. Ideally, winter would be a time to curl up with a good book for hours, even days, on end. But when winter hits, I am more likely to pace from one end of the house to the other than I am to read.

We all remember the winter of 1997. I am sure the generations to follow will get sick of hearing us tell about it. For the record, I believe there were thirty blizzards that winter. In the end, we had between twelve and fifteen feet of snow. The snow banks were over the treetops. Those of us lucky enough to survive will never forget.

Anyway, I was trapped in my trailer house during one of those blizzards. It was a Saturday night, and it was forty below. Wind gusts were up to forty miles-per-hour, and there was plenty of fresh snow to blow around.

My trailer house felt like solitary confinement. I had to get out of there. To make matters worse, I knew that there was karaoke in town that night. I love to sing karaoke, and getting to town became more important by the minute.

Although I knew it was insane, I jumped in the pickup and took off. Visibility was low. The drifts over the road were hard. There were no tracks visible. I drove the nine miles to town at about thirty miles-per-hour.

Half-way to town, I had regrets. What if I froze to death out there? Was karaoke worth the risk? If I didn't make it, as one of my neighbors once said, the minister would have quite a time making sense out of that one at the funeral.

I pushed on. I arrived to find the parking lot at the karaoke place completely full. I went inside. The place was packed. Apparently quite a few people felt they had to get out of the house. Not a word was said about the blizzard.

A good time was had by all, but I knew that I would wake up one night next summer in a cold sweat, swearing never to drive in such bad weather again.

Depression

According to Ann Landers, October 5 is National Depression Screening Day. You can go in and they'll ask you some questions to see if you might be depressed.

Sounds silly. I mean, do they have a National Eye Exam Day? They probably do, but Ann Landers won't ever mention it, because she doesn't need to. Most people who need glasses or dental work have the good sense to take care of it on their own.

Not so with depression, which in my opinion is as common as tooth decay and near-sightedness. But it is like pulling teeth to get depressed people to seek help.

My mouth is full of fillings. And I've worn eyeglasses since the third grade. Nobody thinks less of me for that.

But if I mention that I've been on anti-depressants for five years and don't intend to go off them any more than I plan to toss my glasses in the lake, well, people look at me like I am a junkie. Who in their right mind would admit they aren't always in their right mind?

People who haven't dealt with depression tend not to understand. They write it off as a fad or as a catch-all excuse. But I would rather have the stomach flu for a month than to have a week of deep depression.

Here's my experience when it gets the worst: You know that sick feeling you get when you meet a cop and realize you are going seventy-five miles-per-hour? That rush of adrenaline?

Now, imagine having that feeling for about eight hours per day without a reason. For weeks. Nothing gets rid of it. You can run three miles and it doesn't go away. The body just keeps producing whatever juice it is that gives you that sick feeling in the gut.

Doctors call that sick feeling anxiety. But it can arise from depression. There are other stages and symptoms. Some people no longer enjoy reading the paper, or other hobbies. They sleep all the time. They hide in their house. It takes them a day to recover from a visit to the local cafe.

I know it's getting bad when I see happy people and instead of envying them, I pity them because they are too stupid to understand the utter futility of life. Poor things! They don't know how bad they have it.

Depression is hereditary. I won't say that every time I climb the family tree I find more nuts, but I do find brilliant people who were often completely debilitated by sadness and a sense of failure.

Worst of all, depression is contagious. Living with a depressed person is hell. It drags everybody down.

Winter is the worst for many people. For me, bright lights help. Arizona provides an instant cure. But if I stay here in the cold, I keep taking pills which help tilt the balance of the brain chemicals towards greater calm.

They work, and they aren't hard to get.

CHAPTER EIGHT

TRAVEL

~

Vacation Dilemma

A person is supposed to take a summer vacation, but where to? The mountains? The lakes? We're supposed to get away from it all, but how do I get away from it all when I am not sure where it all is?

I keep postponing my vacation plans because there is just too much to do at home. We have such short summers, why not enjoy them? Stuff is blooming. The grass needs frequent mowing.

Going to the lake does not appeal to me. I water-skied once. The thermometer said 49 degrees. I made it out of the water and did fine until the first turn, when I tripped on the wake and went down. Water up the nose. Never again.

Sitting on the beach at a lake is anything but peaceful with all of those personal water craft, or whatever those snowmobiles on water are called, buzzing around. No fun there.

Camping in the mountains might be a possibility if I could hire somebody to remember everything for me. Last time I camped in the mountains, I forgot a rain poncho. It poured for two days.

I thought about driving the Alaskan highway. That's something I have always wanted to do. What an adventure, driving through the Yukon, seeing the midnight sun.

But really, is that a vacation, driving 3200 miles one-way to Anchorage? That's one oil change just to get where you're going. And then you are 3200 miles from home with no way to get back but to drive the way you came.

My frequent flier miles have built up to the point where I could fly free to England courtesy of Northwest Airlines. Hey, I thought, I have always wanted to hike the moors up by York.

Hiking in England is great. Not only do they have good walking trails, but they have bed and breakfasts evenly spaced along the way. No need for a tent. No dehydrated food. No sleeping bags. Sounds like my kind of hike.

Well, I did a little research and found that all the walking trails in England are closed this summer. Seems many of them run through cow pastures. Walkers might spread or catch hoof-and-mouth disease.

So, diseased cows kaboshed my grandest summer vacation idea.

By process of elimination, I have narrowed it down to Itasca Park. That really makes the most sense. I will leave home about two o'clock in the afternoon one day in August. I will hike a short trail, and climb that fire tower.

I will then eat a nice meal at Douglas Lodge. On the way out, I will stop by the headwaters to walk across those rocks and think profound thoughts about the Mississippi River. Thoughts like: Who decided that this little stream was the headwaters of the Mississippi instead of some little ditch in Wisconsin? Or Montana? Or Ohio?

Then I will head home, arriving just after dark, to my own bed, my own coffee maker, and my own cereal dishes. Vacation complete.

Planes and Trains

I enjoy New York, but I learned last trip not to try to drive there. This time, I took mass transit. In one day, I used six separate forms of transportation.

I drove my pickup to the airport in Minneapolis. I flew to Newark. A shuttle bus carried me into Manhattan where I was dumped off with my luggage at a busy street corner near Penn Station.

I had hoped to store my bag at the train station and explore the city, but thanks to the terrorist scares of some years ago, all lockers had been removed. I was doomed to carry my suitcase all day.

I walked to Grand Central Station. I was shocked to find it sparkling clean. The deep tunnels where bums used to sleep now house wine bars and trendy restaurants which cater to the beautiful people from Wall Street. I think I prefer the bums. I wonder where they are being kept.

I took the subway up to 87th Street on the Upper East Side. I was bound and determined to see an Impressionist exhibit at the Metropolitan Museum of Art. I found the museum, but I never found the Impressionists. Instead, I got lost in the Egyptian heads, which were fascinating enough.

After getting my fill of pharaohs, I set out across Central Park. I should have taken the bus. Central Park is so big that when you are in the middle of it, the city noises are barely audible.

Once I reached the Upper West Side, I called an old college buddy who lived just across the river on the Jersey side. "Just take the ferry across," he said. "I'll pick you up at the dock."

By now, I had undergone as much stress and stimulation in one day as one would in an entire year of living in Norman County. My eyes were tired. I was drenched in sweat. I hated my suitcase.

It was good to see a familiar face at the dock. My college buddy and I shared a time of fellowship and renewal at a little pub before he poured me on the 9:35 train to Princeton, NJ where I spent the weekend with friends.

It was a long day. As I dragged myself off the train, I felt as if I had just staggered off a long ride on the tilt-a-whirl. New York is like that.

I was completely shot, but it was impossible to sleep with the noises of the greatest city on earth still ringing in my ears.

Met Museum

I recently spent a couple of hours at the Metropolitan Museum of Art in New York City. That wasn't long enough, to say the least.

The Met has over two million works of art in its collection. Of that two million, only 100,000 or so are on display at any given time. The rest are stored away somewhere until they get a chance to be displayed.

Do you know how long it would take just to see those 100,000 works of art on display? I figured it out: If I were to spend 10 seconds on each piece, it would take me over a month and a half of eight hour days to get through that small bit of the museum's collection.

If each of the works of art in the Metropolitan's collection is worth, say, one thousand dollars, the whole collection would be worth over two billion dollars. But many of the art works are worth hundreds of thousands of dollars each, and others would likely sell for millions.

I suppose market value is a profane way to measure the value of great art. The Met is packed every day with people from all over the world. There are lines waiting for the place to open up at ten in the morning, even on weekdays, and the visitors aren't there to shop.

I don't know much about art. The word "museum" makes me yawn. I have asked the question many times: How can a painting, any painting, sell for $30 million, as some of Van

Gogh's have? Isn't that as ridiculous as paying somebody $30 million to play one year of basketball?

Who knows. But after I spent an afternoon looking at just a few works of art, I began to appreciate the value art can have for a person's spirit and intellect apart from its staggering dollar value.

As I was ready to leave, I ran across a little carving of gold so delicate and beautiful that I was entranced by it for far longer than the allotted ten seconds. The carving was smaller than a postcard. Some prince has ordered it made for his favorite wife. It took a craftsman years to make.

Carved in the gold was a jungle scene which featured vines intertwined with birds and other animals, all presented in intricate and perfect detail. What amazed me most was that the carving was completed in 8th century Iran. I didn't even realize Iran existed in the 8th century!

Such is the value of a museum. One realizes when one sees the high achievements by artists from thousands of years ago that our modern world is not necessarily the pinnacle of creation. We probably aren't even close to being the richest civilization in history, if one puts any value at all on things of beauty.

Pizza in Brooklyn

The only way to attack New York City as a visitor is to have a goal. Study the subway maps, the train maps, the bus maps, and figure out how to get to that goal.

Once you get to your goal, whether it is a museum, restaurant, concert or a tour—do your thing, then turn around and head back. This seemingly simple process will take you all day and it will wear you to a frazzle. What you see on the journey will keep your mind whirling much of the night.

My goal yesterday was to find Patsy's pizza place in Brooklyn, a little joint which reportedly has the best pizza in New York. It took two hours to reach the general area using the train and the subway. By then, I was starved.

I walked the streets which curl around the base of the Brooklyn Bridge for about a half-hour, passing dozens of pizza places. Lots of chain link fences, razor wire and litter, but no Patsy's.

Too proud to ask directions, I gave up and ducked out of the drizzle into Facciatti's Pizza, where I had some of the best pizza I have ever eaten, for two bucks a slice.

Thus nourished, I set out across the Brooklyn Bridge which, when it was completed in 1875, was regarded as one of the engineering marvels of the world. It is impressive yet today, with many lanes of traffic below and a walkway for pedestrians suspended overhead amongst the cables.

From the bridge's catwalk one sees the length of Manhattan, a wall of buildings running for several miles along the waterfront, most of them forty or fifty stories tall.

To give you an idea of the value of these buildings, there was an advertisement in the New York Times this week for an 8,000 square foot apartment on the Upper East Side. Its asking price? Forty million dollars. For one apartment.

In Minnesota that kind of money could buy you the Metrodome. But in New York it is tough to buy an apartment on the Upper East Side, even a small studio, for under one million dollars.

Why do people live here, you ask? You have to come to New York to understand. The atmosphere is electric. You feel as if you are at the center of civilization. There is something for everybody at any hour of the day or night.

My round trip into the city for pizza took six hours. At its end, back in sleepy New Jersey, I flopped on the bed and stared at the ceiling, utterly shot. Yet, the mental images gathered on the pizza trip would keep me awake for hours.

On paper, New York City sounds like a rat race. But if I was offered the chance to live there for one year of my life, I would snap it up in a heartbeat. The energy of the place makes one feel alive to the fingertips.

Jersey Manners

While staying with friends on the east coast in a bedroom community only a short train ride from New York City, I have been able to glimpse an entirely different culture.

Midwesterners are prone to think Easterners are rude, but I beg to differ. East coasters are louder than Midwesterners, more willing to say what they think, and more likely to tell you to get out of their way. But if you need help, they'll be there just as surely as good, solid Midwesterners.

The first thing I did after crossing the New Jersey border was lock my keys in my pickup at an exit off the New Jersey turnpike. I walked to a gas station with bars on its windows. The attendants looked surly.

I asked what to do, should I call the cops? "No, forghedaboudit," the attendant said in his Joisey accent. "Da boys in da back can take care of it."

Out came two gangster-like guys with baggy pants, funny hats and a couple of tools. They should be experts at getting into locked cars, I thought.

They weren't. Although they had been in a big fight the night before, which they described to me in great detail, they weren't car thieves. It took them twenty minutes to open my pickup. Several times I offered to call the police, but they said no, we'll get it.

When they finished, I was so grateful and relieved that I pulled out every small bill in my wallet. The gangster good samaritans didn't bother going through the Minnesota ritual of trying to turn money down. No, they snatched it, said thanks, and were off.

So, my first encounter with people from the east coast went smoothly, as has every other one since, and on past trips. People are helpful. People hold the doors for others. They yell a lot, their language is routinely salty, they are in a hurry, but they are basically friendly.

The topography in New Jersey is not that different from that of Minnesota's lake country. Woods, ponds, corn fields. But if you squint hard as you look through the woods, you can see a housing development or a shopping mall on the other side.

The population is dense. The highways are crowded. The stores are full. As you get closer to New York City, it gets worse.

To survive in this crowded environment, one must be a little pushy. People put their heads down and plow forward at full speed, or they'll likely get run over themselves.

That said, people out here are very understanding of each other. Everybody's in a hurry, so it's no big deal when people are pushy or rude. It's par for the course. And from what I've seen, if East Coasters have a chance to help you out, they'll do so quickly, then get on their way and out of yours.

Jersey Barber Shop

A trip to the barber shop is a good way to get a feel for a local culture, if you can even find an actual barber shop these days.

Most old-time barbers named Herb or Mel have died and have been replaced by "stylists" named Amanda or Jeremy. The striped barber's pole has been replaced by neon signs with salon names like "The Hair Affair," or "Klips and Kutz."

But on the main street of a little central New Jersey town, I found a striped barber pole. My hair was shaggy, so I walked in. Dick the friendly barber said, "Sit down, you're next."

Dick's shop had only one chair. The waiting area was empty. The *Field and Stream* magazines were two years old and crinkled. Dick was obviously close to retirement, a relic of the past, a Model T in a world of Toyota Camrys.

But as Dick stretched the crepe paper around my neck, I shut my eyes and imagined I was back in 1950s New Jersey. I pictured the tattered armchairs filled with pipe-smoking, slick-haired men waiting their turn.

Dick noticed my accent and asked where I was from. I told him, but he had no interest in Minnesota. Like any local person anywhere, all he wanted to know was, "What do you think of central New Jersey?"

I said nice things. I said I thought the people were friendly. I said I enjoyed being so close to New York City, and that I thought the people in the city were friendly and helpful, too, despite all I had been told.

"Just don't go to Philadelphia," Dick said. "Those people are rude."

That was news to me, but then I remembered that Philadelphia sports fans have a reputation as the nastiest spectators in the country. Dick agreed.

"During the subway World Series in New York, there was not one fan arrested, not one!" he said with pride. "And they hate each other."

But at Veteran's Stadium in Philadelphia, Dick reported, things are so bad that they have a courtroom in the basement with a real county judge who tries cases of disorderly conduct, drunkenness and assault right on the spot.

No sir, he said, New Yorkers are saints when compared to people from the City of Brotherly Love.

We went on to other traditional barber shop topics. Taxes. Government conspiracies. Boxing. Rigged football games. Cars.

Finally, Dick slapped some hot shaving cream on my neck, shaved it with a straight-edge razor, and handed me my glasses. My fifteen minute trip back to the 1950s was over.

When I walked out the door, I took a closer look at the striped barber poll. As it spun around, I got a cruel jolt into the present: Between the stripes was printed the word "stylist." Dick wasn't a barber after all.

Oasis in Kentucky

Last week's winter storm nipped at my heels for three days as I drove from northern Minnesota to the heart of Dixie. Bad driving conditions finally forced me off the freeway in Kentucky, which had its last major snow storm in 1993.

Thinking that one motel is as good as the next, I took the one with the $33.95 sign. Turns out that price is good only if you have a coupon, are a certified businessman, are very old, or are a member of the military. I was too tired to lie, so after tax, the bill came to $46.45.

The hotel had no inside stairwell. The outside stairs were covered in snow. The room was tiny with a huge window covered by frost. On the condensation-drenched window sill was a Gideon Bible, opened to the book of Job.

The heater in room 226 gave you two choices, sauna or deep freeze. I alternated throughout the night. The sheets were clean, but something told me that the bedspread was last laundered several truckers ago. The bathroom fan sounded like a coffee grinder.

After getting settled, I set out into the storm to find a restaurant. I trudged through the ankle-deep slush, across intersections designed more for semis than pedestrians, along frontage roads without sidewalks.

I hoped for a Denny's, Perkins, Pizza Hut, it didn't matter. But lo and behold, through the falling snow I spotted a dimly lit sign: "Feast of India." My favorite cuisine! I couldn't believe my luck.

Indian restaurants, although most of them are called "Feast of India," are each unique. There are so many different ways to prepare the basic Indian dishes that no two Feasts of India ever turn out alike.

As is my custom, I asked the waiter with the biggest turban to help me choose a good dish. He shook his head. Eveddyting on the menu is veddy, veddy good, he said.

I pointed to number forty-seven. Number forty-seven is veddy good, he said. I pointed to another. Number fifty-nine is also veddy good, as is number seventy-two. Eveddyting is veddy good.

So, I asked, which would you recommend of the three? Number thirty-nine, he said. His steely glare made me hesitate to point out that thirty-nine wasn't on my original list.

I ordered thirty-nine, and asked him to make it medium hot. Medium hot in an Indian restaurant is spicy enough to make your scalp tingle, your sinuses empty, and your chest clear.

Indian food is great, but the most enjoyable dishes are those which provide an excuse to dip into the sauces. Indian sauces are vivid, ranging from cool to hot, from spicy to sweet, from fresh to fermented.

After I finished, the waiter asked if eveddyting was okay. I couldn't resist. I said the meal was veddy, veddy good. In fact, I said with a thumbs up sign, eveddyting was absolutely atrocious.

He liked that, and sent me off to my cheap motel with a big smile, two mint toothpicks, and a warm feeling of cross-cultural understanding.

Florida

Greetings from Miami, FL, the land of peeling pink and turquoise paint. Miami is one of those places I would never go unless I had a friend there with an extra room.

That extra room is in a neighborhood filled with palms, beautiful wild parrots, green grass and attractive apartment buildings. Looks great, but there are certain streets I have been warned not turn down lest I end up as a statistic.

Oh well. The weather seems warm, to me at least. Last week temperatures plunged into the lower sixties, which brought on a loud round of complaining at the local cafe. While taking walks, I have been bawled out by no fewer than five Jewish grandmothers for not wearing a cap.

Yes, they have a local breakfast cafe here. Karen the owner, whose hair is dyed the same brownish red used by so many women around here, serves twelve types of bagels. The old men talk about condo deals, stock scams and interest rates, not machinery and crops.

When I visited New York City, I wondered what happens to people when they get too old and decrepit to keep up with the frantic pace of life there.

Turns out, New York sends its cigar-chomping retired men and their red-haired wives to Miami, where they are outfitted with brightly colored polyester slacks and stacked up in high rise condos.

Take a walk down a Miami street in the evening. Through

the open windows of the condos you will overhear dozens of half-deaf New Yorkers conversing with their spouses in a tone of voice which would bring a visit from the county social worker in the Midwest.

People yell at people they know, they yell at people they don't know. They yell at waiters and waitresses. They yell at the parking attendant. My nerves get frayed from all the yelling, but nobody else seems to care.

I have heard of funeral pre-planning. In Miami, it seems that many of the people have been pre-embalmed. Caked on make-up. Dyed hair, fake hair, purple hair. Heavy carnation-scented perfumes. An unusually high toupee-per-capita ratio.

There's nothing more hideous than people with too much money who refuse to age gracefully, who try to convince themselves with hair dyes and facelifts that they are still thirty.

But retirees are only part of Miami. Go down to the beach, and you will see mile after mile of tantalizing sights it would be unwise to describe here. You will hear languages from all over the world.

On the sidewalk in front of an Italian cafe, I paused by a table jammed with four generations of a large Italian family, all talking at the same time, in Italian, waving their hands, eating pasta, and rolling their r's—a delightful scene straight out of a movie.

Miami is unlike any place I have ever been. Best of all, it can be viewed in a t-shirt and shorts, on foot, and in January. There's a lot to be said for that.

Escape from Miami

Big bookstores are the highlight of my vacations, but to get to one in Miami I had to cut across eight lanes of Miami traffic. In fact, to get anywhere in Miami you have to cut across eight lanes of traffic.

Miami traffic is a nightmarish combination of slow moving retirees, crazy driving immigrants accustomed to the rules of some other country, and people on various substances fleeing from the police helicopters overhead. It makes one frazzled.

When I finally got to the bookstore, it was anything but a refuge. It was crowded with people, many of them talking on cell phones. All of the big soft chairs were full. There was a long line at the coffee shop.

About this time, I said to myself, am I having fun? Is Miami the vacation spot for me?

The answer was clearly no, and within an hour I said thanks to my gracious host, randomly stuffed my junk in duffle bags and headed north on I-95 as fast as the traffic would allow.

Florida is one big swamp. Literally and morally. The first billboard which greets you when you cross the state line says "We dare bare all!" It is an advertisement for Cafe Erotica. Great food! Adult videos! All in one location. Bon appetit.

It goes downhill from there. Figuratively speaking, of course, for there are no hills in Florida. The whole place is about ten feet above sea level. If global warming melts the arctic ice cap, let's just say that our future elections will run a lot more smoothly.

After escaping Miami, I made it as far north as Daytona Beach. Motel rooms for $12.88. Good deal, I thought, although I decided to be safe and take a $25 room.

Bad move. The stench was amazing. The phone did not work. The air conditioner rattled even though it was off. There were cigarette burns all over the bedspread.

Did I say stench? Let me tell you, do not go into restrooms in a gas station in Florida unless they advertise on a huge billboard, "Clean Restrooms!" By gum, if a gas station down here goes through the trouble of cleaning their restrooms, they will advertise it big.

At the rest areas they have replaced janitors with armed guards. So, you are safe against crime but completely vulnerable to hepatitis A through L.

Billboards, billboards, billboards. Vasectomy reversals. Gentleman's Club, next exit. See the world's largest alligator! Hurt in an accident? We can help, call 1-800-SNAKE.

The crowning incident happened while I was in a big department store. An old man fell in the suit section. He was fine, it seemed, a little shook up. But what did the clerk do? Ask him if he was okay?

No, she ignored the man and called the manager, who angrily informed the man that he had to leave the store. "We cannot risk having somebody who falls around here," he said.

This is Florida, land of snakes, alligators and lawyers, a place which could benefit from a whole army of Lutheran missionaries, if the Lutherans still do that sort of thing.

Georgia

I have taken refuge in the mountains north of Atlanta. Georgia winter weather is like October weather in northern Minnesota. In other words, it's about perfect.

Atlanta is an expanding metropolis. Developers are pushing deep into the wooded mountains forty miles from downtown.

Yet, between spanking new subdivisions like Foxtrot Estates and Woodlawn Grove, one can still find run-down shacks nestled deep in a ravine, enshrouded in a cloud of wood smoke, surrounded by rusted cars and farm equipment.

The new subdivisions are home to vice presidents of marketing and directors of sales, many with Northern accents. The shacks are home to drawling old locals whose memory of the Civil War is as fresh as yesterday.

Now, I admit to prejudice against people with deep southern drawls. I tend to doubt their intelligence. I wonder about their prejudices. I worry about my safety.

When you think of it, the only exposure we northern Minnesotans get to people from the deep South comes when the carnival pulls into town for the county fair. When I hear a southern accent, my first reaction is to grab for my wallet and walk fast.

What are the images of Southerners on television? We see them as the drawling racists on civil rights documentaries, or the con-artist evangelists on cable, or the trailer park trash fighting it out on Jerry Springer.

None of my experience here has justified my prejudices. What I have found instead is a quiet politeness, a warm hospitality, and a friendly openness.

In Miami, it was noise, noise, noise, even in bookstores. Here in the Old South, manners still seem important. People even have the grace to step outside the bookstore coffee shop before they talk on their cellular phones.

Sure, at a low class rib joint you're liable to hear some loud conversation. At Denny's the waitresses might loudly complain to each other about husband Bubba's beer drinkin. But for the most part, a gentle politeness prevails.

And the food. What we call hotdishes, Southerners call casseroles. Local diners offer a wide selection of casseroles, plus your choice of rutabagas, okra, corn, or black-eyed peas, topped off with a biscuit or cornbread.

Doug's Place is a ramshackle back country restaurant with a tin roof, a dozen lean-to additions, sloped floors partially covered with decades-old linoleum, and chairs that don't sit straight. The menu is typed up new every morning and gives you the choice of fifteen casseroles.

I chose numbers three, seven, and twelve and in less than three minutes I had a plate of food in front of me as hearty as anything I've eaten in a Minnesota church basement.

Such food goes a long way towards making one feel at home in this foreign land of Georgia.

Atlanta Adventure

A small ad in the Atlanta paper last week announced a pipe organ concert at a downtown church. On a whim I decided to drive into the city to take it in, not knowing what I was getting into.

Pipe organ concerts in this country tend to draw sparse crowds of dandruff-sprinkled eccentrics. But hundreds jammed St. Luke's Episcopal Church to bask in the roar of an instrument with five keyboards, 5,000 pipes, a tooth-rattling rumble in the loud parts and soft sounds that would melt butter.

After the concert, I turned to a gentleman in the pew next to me and said, you know, I don't think I have ever heard a finer pipe organ sound. My accent gave me away as a foreigner and the man asked me to explain my origins.

Something about a compliment from a visitor from Minnesota got the ball rolling. Although I was dressed in ripped jeans and a T-shirt, the gentleman dragged me back to the gala black tie champagne reception and had me repeat my comments to the hoity toities who put up the millions for the renovation.

Well, what did I have to lose? I decided to have fun. I bragged about the acoustics of the room and the effects of the wooden ceiling on the tone of the bass pipes. The dignified Southern matrons ate it up and egged me on.

I didn't see the organist listening in. A gracious Southern gentleman, he said, well then, you must come play the organ.

Oops. Having me play that monster is like sending an ultra-light pilot into the cockpit of a 747. But how could I say no? If nothing else, I wanted to pull out all the stops, hit a simple chord, and feel the rumble.

I hoped to sneak in the sanctuary, hit a few notes and then leave, but when I arrived at my appointed hour, not only was the organist waiting, but a couple of the parishioners showed up as well.

Apparently my compliments, all of them sincere, had convinced these people that I actually knew how to play. They were proud of their wonderful organ and wanted to hear this refugee from Lake Wobegon air it out.

I took a deep breath, hit the button that pulls out all the stops, and played my little Bach piece with as much bluster and gusto as I could muster. It was a thrill of a lifetime for me, but they wanted to hear more. So I played the same piece again, but louder. And again.

Finally satisfied that I didn't know anything else, the audience left. Thinking I was alone, I played "What a Friend We Have in Jesus" and "Take Me Out to the Ball Game" over and over, trying out as many of the hundreds of stops as I could. Occasionally, I pulled out all the stops and hit a low bass note just to hear the chandeliers rattle. After two hours, I finally quit.

Turns out I hadn't been alone. As I walked past the church secretaries, it was clear that they had their fill of "What a Friend We have in Jesus" at full volume. They seemed happy to find out I was from Minnesota and was planning to return there soon.

Dixie Doodles

After my trip south, I stopped to think: What do we have in the North, in particular in the far upper Midwest, that makes living here worthwhile, despite the cold weather?

A few things: Clean rest areas. Motels that don't stink. Businesses which take checks. Open spaces and wide side roads. Reasonably polite drivers.

Less smoking in public places. Less corruption, public and private. A feeling of safety. Less litter on the roadside. People who take pride in their yards.

Good singers. I sang karaoke in rural Florida. What a disaster. Nobody down there could carry a tune. Up north, thanks perhaps to what is left of the great Lutheran choral tradition, karaoke bars draw real talent.

Speaking of Lutherans: In Cartersville, GA, population 80,000, there are 73 Baptist churches, dozens of Methodist, Presbyterian and Pentecostal churches, but only one Lutheran church and one Catholic church. Lutherans and Catholics are such a hopeless minority nobody even bothers to persecute them.

History. Miami has little history before 1920. Just as Phoenix was a small town before air conditioning, Miami was a mere hamlet before DDT controlled the insects. After the war, the population of both cities exploded. Yet, there is something lacking in the character of young cities populated by people who have fled their roots.

We have an average of four generations of history in northwest Minnesota, which is about right. Any more and we'd fight each other like they do in Eastern Europe. But it's good to maintain enough of our heritage to prevent lefse from going extinct.

Stop lights which turn green. In the south, they time the lights so you could have a nap, snarf down a taco, read the paper and brush your teeth before the green left turn arrow turns. No wonder Southerners run red lights with abandon. Stopping means adding ten minutes to your trip.

What do we miss out on up here in the north, besides warmth?

I enjoyed the established Latin culture in Miami, as I always have in Arizona. I enjoyed hearing dozens of languages and sampling obscure foods. I had never heard of Chinese-Cuban food or tasted Chilean fare, but both were sure good.

Georgia had a wonderful history, most vividly illustrated for me by a narrow country lane I saw lined by 200-year-old oak trees which somebody long ago had planted. You don't see old oak in rows up here.

Because there is so little freezing and thawing, the roads in the South don't have those cracks that have to be filled by stripes of black goop. Trips on the freeway and the side roads are blissfully smooth, just like on a fresh stretch of tar up here.

South Florida is unfriendly, but the Old South is brimming with hospitality and warmth. I kind of enjoyed being called honey. If I ever got called honey by a waitress up here, I think my teeth would fall into my soup. And I still have my real ones.

As much as I loathe the cold, I suppose it is good to get back north in time to endure some of it. Otherwise, my character might start deteriorating and I might qualify as riff-raff.

Sherman Lives

They're still furious with Sherman in Atlanta. A recent letter to the editor of the Atlanta paper proclaimed, "Sherman should have hung with the rest of the war criminals." Poor Sherman is denounced in such terms almost weekly.

Sherman who, you say? They're referring to William Tecumseh Sherman, the great Civil War Union general who fought his way to Atlanta with 100,000 men and captured the city from the Confederacy in 1864.

Some history: Sherman wasn't pleased to possess Atlanta. The Confederate armies escaped him. Sherman was now stuck holding onto the city and trying to manage its residents, which he regarded as a waste of his talent and his men's time.

So, Sherman allowed the people of Atlanta a few days to evacuate either north or south, and burnt the place to the ground.

For those familiar with the brutal twentieth century wars, taking a war to the people doesn't seem unusual. But in the nineteenth century, burning a city was regarded as ungentlemanly behavior. There still is the sense in Georgia that yes, the South lost the war, but Sherman didn't have to rub it in.

I visited an Episcopal Church in Atlanta a couple of weeks back. One of the first things the parishioners told me was, "Of course, Sherman burnt the original building to the ground." The church members were very proud of the two stained glass windows salvaged from the fire.

I didn't mention to the Georgians that I spent my spare time on my visit reading Sherman's memoirs to get his side of the story.

Sherman is quick to point out that no citizens were killed, that the evacuation of Atlanta was humane, and that the people were fed. He figured that since it was futile to try to corner and defeat the fast-moving Confederate armies, you had just as well ruin their property. "War is hell," he said. If you don't like it, surrender.

To that end, Sherman though it prudent to burn "all buildings which could be turned to military uses" in Atlanta. Apparently the Episcopal Church qualified, as did nearly every other public building. Sherman then left Atlanta in ruins and burnt his way 300 miles to the sea.

To this day, Atlantans feel Sherman vandalized their history and stole their heritage. Other cities in the Old South have wonderful pre-Civil War downtowns which are now restored into tourist attractions. Atlanta has none.

Over the hill from where I stayed in Georgia there stands a stately old house which, I found out, Sherman ordered his men to spare. It is still occupied, and in good shape.

Why was that house saved when so much else was burned? Well, Sherman found out the house was owned by General Grant's niece. He decided the Union could afford to let it stand.

Montana Drivers

Boy, it sure is tough for these people in Montana. Their legislature is always digging up new ways to spoil their fun.

For instance, if you decide to spend an evening at the Deerlick Saloon, the state mandates that you have to leave the bar by sunrise. Can you imagine.

Fortunately, if you haven't finished your most recent beverage, you are free to bring it, and a couple more if you wish, along with you and drink up in your pickup truck. You can't be drunk while driving, but you are free to work on it.

A couple of years ago, the Montana legislature came up with the crazy idea of limiting the speed people can drive on Montana highways. Their feeble excuse was that foreigners were descending upon the state to race their Ferraris and Porsches down the interstate.

Nothing wrong with races on I-90, except these stupid out-of-staters couldn't keep their Ferraris and Porsches on the road. When they flew end-over-end off the highway at 135 miles-per-hour, their cars became a danger to livestock and sheepdogs. So, now Montana has a speed limit.

To their credit, most Montanans completely ignore the new law.

Montana is said to have beautiful scenery. I wouldn't know. The mountains and streams fade to a blur as I race to keep up with traffic on these curvy mountain roads. Most Montana residents seem happy to risk the $5 fine that comes from getting stopped for doing ninety.

Ever tried to be calm and collected with a logging truck 20 yards off your tail—and you are already doing eighty?

The pickup trucks with multiple gun racks—well, they are a little slow. Seems their owners are too busy scanning the ditches for fox, deer, minorities, and jackrabbits.

But watch out for young mothers in minivans with "Jesus Saves" bumper stickers. They stop for nothing, especially if Pampers are on sale at the Kmart in Missoula. Feel a tap from behind and you had better pull over to let them through.

Despite their repressive and tyrannical laws, the Montana legislature does have one soft spot for its drivers:

If, through no fault of your own, you fly off a hairpin curve at ninety miles-per-hour, you are immediately declared a Montana "Hero of the Highway" and given your very own steel cross marker, right at the spot where you went over the edge. If you brought others with you, they get crosses, too.

If you are real lucky, your surviving kinfolk will run out to Wal-mart and buy a purty plastic wreath of flowers to hang on cross. The cross and the flowers will stand as a lasting memorial—until somebody runs them over on their way over the same cliff.

I drive too fast on the highway to know for sure, but it seems that there is a cross, or a set of crosses, every couple of miles. It's really kind of touching. It can't be easy to mow around all of those things.

Montana Mountains

It has been ten years since I have traveled west into Montana. Last week I decided it was time to see the mountains again.

On family vacations when I was a child, I looked forward to seeing the mountains as much as I might look forward to seeing a Twins game.

As we crept west across the prairie in the LTD station wagon, I kept my eyes peeled for mountains in the distance. I usually began to see snow-capped peaks on the horizon just west of Bismarck. Of course, those mountains always turned out to be clouds. Or a mirage.

When we reached Billings a day later, we finally could make out in the distance the snow fields of the Beartooth range to the south.

As we drove closer, the mountains looked ominous, foreboding. Thunderstorms hovered over the ranges in the afternoons. The sheer cliffs seemed scary to a child of the prairie, but seeing them thrilled me all the same.

One wonders, what is it about mountains that is so alluring, that draws thousands of people thousands of miles? Perhaps it is the combination of beauty and danger which makes mountains so irresistible.

Montana crawls with tourists each summer, and most of them won't bait a line or walk a trail. They come to see the mountains.

I have often wondered, do people who live near mountains get used to them and take them for granted?

My great-grandmother came across from Norway. Although she was happy here and loved her little house in Twin Valley, MN, she once said that the only thing missing in her new country was a mountain out back.

Mountains have mystical power. Many Indian tribes consider them sacred. Some people talk about mountains as if they were friends. An Old Testament figure once said "I look to the mountains, from whence cometh my strength."

Seems like an odd statement, until one drives between two mountain ranges, through one of Montana's grand valleys. From the highway, the line of sight extends up to fifty miles in every direction. Within that view stand millions of trees and dozens of snow-covered peaks.

Those mountains have towered there for thousands of years, virtually unchanged. They stood there before we arrived, and they'll be there long after we are gone.

Such alpine grandeur might make one feel overwhelmed, dwarfed, belittled. But I felt nothing of the sort, and I don't think others who visit the mountains do either.

Instead, by reminding us of our smallness, these mountain vistas give us a perspective we lack back at the office, a perspective as broad as the Montana sky. Mountain scenes refresh the spirit and calm the mind. Mountain air invigorates the imagination.

No wonder western Montana crawls with immigrants from the city—tourists, artists, and others who seek relief from the fatigue of life on the treadmill. They've cometh to the mountains to getteth some strength.

Livingston, MT

Livingston, Montana is infamous for its truck-flipping gusts. When the winds pick up, the stretch of I-90 which passes through the town becomes truly hazardous, particularly to top-heavy semi-trailers.

Livingston sits just north of the grand Paradise Valley. Through the middle of the valley runs the Yellowstone River. In the valley on either side of the river are pasture and irrigated fields of alfalfa. The movie "A River Runs Through It" was filmed there.

Some of the grandest snow-capped peaks in Montana surround the enormous valley. It is no wonder that amongst the cows, alfalfa, rustic barns and farm homes, new mansions for movie stars and retired ballplayers pop up almost weekly.

As a child of the prairie, I found the wide open spaces and crops of the Paradise Valley to be a comfort. The narrow mountain gorges in other parts of Montana make me claustrophobic. I enjoy a mountain range more when it is set behind about a thousand acres of round bales, or maybe a quarter section of wheat.

Livingston is at 4500 feet. It seems that at such high elevations, the sky becomes a darker blue, the colors deepen, and you can see twice the stars—all without the benefit of mood altering substances. Elevation alone can be a natural high.

Paradise Valley is twenty to thirty miles wide and about sixty miles long. At its north end, the broad valley narrows into a small gap through which runs the Yellowstone River.

Hence the wind in Livingston, a little town perched just north of that small gap. The gentle breezes from the valley gain frightening force as they funnel through the small aperture at the valley's northern end, blasting Livingston and the transcontinental truck traffic on I-90.

Perhaps the wind is why Livingston has remained relatively undiscovered. Few travelers exit the freeway long enough to check out the charming town and the astounding valley to the south.

Downtown Livingston is refurbished and charming, filled with bookstores, art galleries, and good restaurants. Yet a room at the Livingston Super 8 costs no more than the same room might in Jamestown or Glendive.

Meanwhile, the price of a room at the Super 8 in trendy locations like Jackson, WY, or Glacier Park, or West Yellowstone, can run up to $150, even if you are a VIP member of every discount club known to man.

So, I immediately fell for Livingston, despite the wind. The town is civilized enough so you can get a Sunday paper and a good greasy breakfast, yet you can hike in the wild mountains of the Absoraka Range without driving more than fifteen minutes.

The crowds have not yet arrived. For the next ten years or so, Livingston should remain a hidden treasure just off the beaten path.

Bellevue to Butte

Last week I drove from Bellevue, WA to Butte, MT. Both cities lie on I-90 and both start with B, but that's where the similarities end.

Bellevue, across Lake Washington from Seattle, is home to the headquarters of Microsoft. It is a sparkling, spotless, almost antiseptic city, filled with Jaguars, Porsches, and the harried millionaires who drive them.

In Bellevue, a building over ten years old is ripe to be torn down. Fresh looking buildings fall to the wrecking ball to make way for new glass towers twice as tall.

Across the lake in Seattle stands a sparkling new $570 million ballpark, Safeco Field. Safeco is the name of the Bellevue-based insurance company which paid $40 million for the naming rights to the stadium.

I toured the ballpark. The kid in me was thrilled to walk around the field, sit in the dugout, snoop around the clubhouse, visit the press box, and jump up against the fence to see if I was tall enough to pull back a home run.

But the ballpark is more about money than baseball. For $40,000 per year, you can have a season ticket behind home plate. After that, everything is free! Free parking, free gourmet food, free drinks, free scorecards, even. And servants at your elbow. Wow.

Each of the twenty sinks in the clubhouse where the millionaire ballplayers shave is equipped with a dozen brands of shaving cream and a dozen types of razors, laid out neatly in rows. As if those guys can't afford to buy their own razors!

Now, on to Butte, MT. Butte is a mining town, but the mines have closed. The mountains surrounding the city are terraced, clay colored and scarred from mining. Pure ugliness. The boom is long over, and Butte has gone bust.

Butte's downtown features block after block of charming turn-of-the century brick buildings, most of them in advanced stages of decay. The woodwork is gray and rotting. The paint is peeled. Porches sag. The sidewalks are cracked.

Poverty runs rampant in Butte. The water tastes bad and is filled with toxins. Cancer rates are high. The people look exhausted. Two drunks panhandled me outside the dingy Perkins. The only thriving business in town is the sparkling new Wal-Mart superstore.

But you know, I felt at home in Butte. I met a couple of friendly locals. They were fighters, scrapping to make a living, happy in a grim way, defiantly proud of their city, hoping somebody with money and vision comes along who sees potential in all of the old buildings and spruces the place up.

The $570 million that went for a ballpark in Seattle could do wonders for poor Butte! Bellevue has money, but Butte has history, character, grit and charm.

It occurs to me: Aren't the main streets of our little hometowns in northern Minnesota lined with charming, but empty, old buildings? No wonder I felt at home in Butte.

To order additional copies of *Still on the Farm,* send $12.95 (Minnesota residents add $.85 per book sales tax) to: Country Scribe Publishing, 4177 County Highway 1, Fertile, MN 56540.

To order a copy of Bergeson's first book, *Down on the Farm*, a collection of the columns Bergeson wrote during the mid-nineties, send $8.95 (Minnesota residents add $.50 sales tax) to: Country Scribe Publishing, 4177 County Highway 1, Fertile, MN 56540. Supply limited.

To receive Eric Bergeson's weekly column via e-mail, write him at ericberg@gvtel.com.